COPYRIGHT

LIMITATION OF LIABILITY

Introduction to IT Principles

Before working through this *IT Principles* Resource Pack it is important that you read the following information that has been written to offer you guidance on how to get the best from it.

The resource pack has been divided into units. Each unit consists of a number of IT related categories. Throughout these categories are tasks, designed to help you understand how to use the computer and how the different parts of a computer work.

At your own pace, you are required to read through the resource pack, learning about different aspects of the computer and how it is used to help understand the important and basic principles of Information Technology.

At key moments throughout the resource pack you will be instructed to perform a practical assignment or task. These tasks are there to demonstrate with a practical hands-on approach the important theoretical aspects of the computer that might otherwise be difficult to understand by merely reading through the resource pack.

It is important that you carefully read through each category before attempting to do the tasks, as this will equip you with the knowledge you will need to answer the questions contained within each task.

Don't worry if occasionally you find yourself having to refer to the section you have just read in order to complete a task. Only through reading each category and completing the accompanying tasks will you correctly learn about the principles of IT.

Consolidation exercises are also contained within each resource pack. These exercises provide a further opportunity to recap the various categories and tasks that you will have previously undertaken while earlier working through the resource pack.

By following these simple instructions and correctly using this resource pack, you will find that learning about the principles of IT will be far more enjoyable and so much easier.

IT Principles

The IT Principles Resource Pack will enable you to perform the most basic operations on a computer, from starting the computer to managing the files and folders contained within it.

You will learn how to manage the Windows environment and seek help when required. You will learn about the devices that can work with a computer such as the keyboard, mouse and printer.

The resource pack covers the Windows Explorer file management system together with the My Computer management system and basic word processing functions using Microsoft Word 2000. Additionally you will learn about the various storage devices, networks, communication methods (e-mail), Health and Safety and security.

Contents

Closing Documents

Open Existing Documents

Spelling And Grammar

Sorting Files

UNIT 5

Creating Folders (Directories) In Windows Explorer

Renaming Files And Folders

UNIT 6

File Management Within My Computer

Changing Views

Creating Folders (Directories) In My Computer

On completion of this unit you will have learnt about:

Basic Operations
- Starting The Computer
- The Desktop Environment
- Shutting Down And Switching Off The Computer
- Restarting The Computer
- Quit A Program That Is Not Responding
- Shutting Down The Computer When It 'Hangs'
- View The System Information
- The Taskbar And Start Button
- Settings

Windows
- How to Switch Between Programs (Applications)
- Switch Between Separate Documents In The Same Application
- Scale An Application Window
- Resize An Application Window
- Move An Application Window
- Search

Help!
- How To Use The Help Function
- Run
- View The Desktop Configuration
- Volume Settings

Input Devices
- Mouse/Pointer Device
- Keyboard
- Scanner
- The Keyboard In Detail

Output Devices
- Monitor/VDU (Visual Display Unit)
- Pixel
- Resolution
- Display Properties
- Desktop Display Options
- Background
- Screen Saver
- Desktop Settings
- Appearance
- Printers
- Speakers
- The Personal Computer

System Unit
- CPU
- Hard Disk And Power Supply
- Support Chips
- Expansion Boards
- Bus

Basic Operations

Starting The Computer

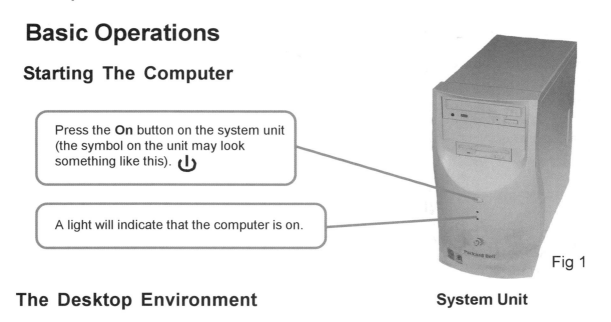

Press the **On** button on the system unit (the symbol on the unit may look something like this). ⏻

A light will indicate that the computer is on.

Fig 1

The Desktop Environment

System Unit

What Is A Desktop?

The **Desktop** in relation to the computer is similar to the top of your own desk. On your desktop you tend to place items that you use regularly, such as a stapler, hole punch or phone. The computer **Desktop** is the initial screen that appears when your computer has started up. It may appear similar to the screen in Fig 2.

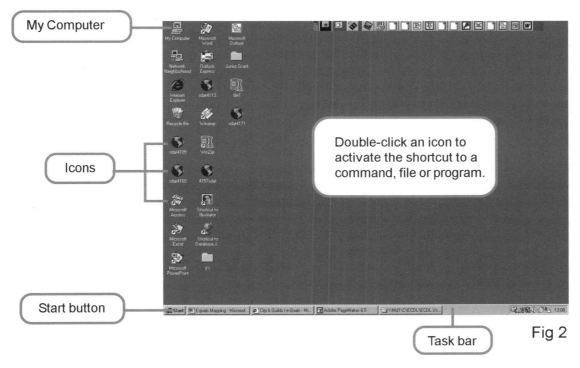

My Computer

Icons

Double-click an icon to activate the shortcut to a command, file or program.

Start button

Task bar

Fig 2

The computer **Desktop** has icons (pictures) on it. Icons represent objects or programs.

Icons of regularly used items are placed on the **Desktop** to make it quicker to access files or programs. Double clicking on an icon will start the program it is associated with or open the file that the icon represents.

However, having too many icons on the **Desktop** can make it cluttered, just as having too many items on your desk would make it difficult to find a piece of work.

Shutting Down And Switching Off The Computer

The computer must be shut down correctly, or else data may be lost, or damage to the hard disk may occur.
The correct shut down procedure is:
Save and close any open documents and close all applications.

Click **Start.**
Click **Shut down**.

Ensure **Shut down** is displayed
(if the **Shut down** option is not showing, click on the drop-down arrow and select it from the list).
Click **OK.**

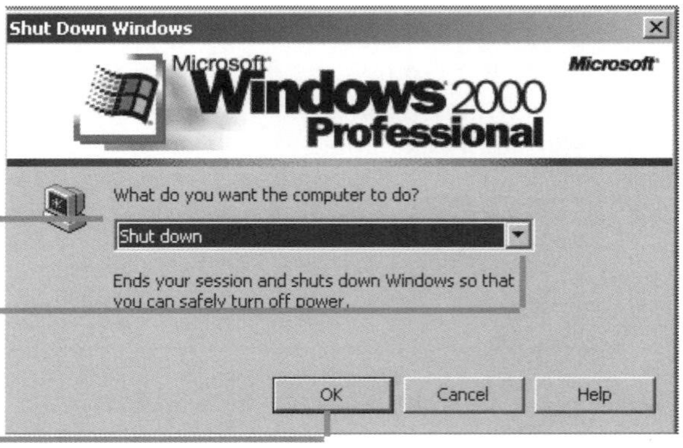

Fig 3

The computer has now been shut down.

NB If you turn off your computer from the system unit without shutting it down correctly, you risk losing information. If your computer doesn't turn off automatically, a message will appear on your screeen to tell you when it can be safely turned off.

Restarting The Computer

To save any new settings you have made or when adding a new piece of hardware you can restart your computer without actually switching it off. Restarting the computer saves any Windows settings that you have changed, and then restarts your computer. When starting the computer ensure that any floppy disks you have been working with are not still in the floppy disk drive.

Click **Start**.
Click **Shut down**.

Click on the drop-down arrow.

Select **Restart**.

Click **OK**.

Fig 4

Quit A Program That Is Not Responding

Sometimes an application freezes, which stops it from responding to your commands.

Press and hold the **Ctrl+Alt** keys then press the **Delete** key (whilst still holding the Ctrl+Alt keys).

The **Windows Security** dialogue box will then appear. Click the **Task Manager** button to display the **Windows Task Manager** dialogue box as shown in Fig 5.

All the applications and documents that are currently open on the computer will then be listed.

Select the document or application that is not responding and click the **End Task** button.

The selected document will now be closed down and will disappear from the list.

It has not been deleted but closed down and can be re-opened at any time.

Fig 5

Shutting Down The Computer When It 'Hangs'

Sometimes the computer 'hangs' on a screen, which stops it from responding to your commands. If you cannot solve this using the above method, follow the steps below to force the computer to shut down and restart.

Press the **Ctrl+Alt** keys and press the **Delete** key twice.

This will restart the computer, checking and mending any resulting errors.

NB If the computer does not respond to the above procedures, the computer will have to be switched off without being closed down correctly. This is usually achieved by depressing the power button on the front of the system unit until the computer switches off. Switch on the computer and after a few seconds shut down the computer correctly, to ensure resulting errors from 'hanging' have been rectified. Switch on the computer to use as normal.

View The System Information

The Microsoft **System Information** displays information such as the:

- Operating environment (eg Microsoft Windows 2000 Professional).
- Processor type and speed.
- Amount of Memory installed.
- Available hard drive space (space for saving).

The following sequence of instructions will provide you with access to the Microsoft System Information dialogue box.

Click **Start**.
Click **Programs**.
Click **Accessories**.
Click **System Tools**.
Click **System Information**.

The **System Information** should then be displayed as illustrated in Fig 6.

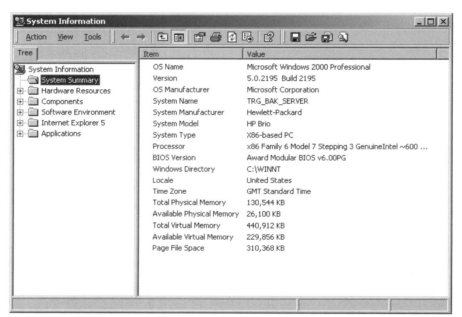

Fig 6

Clicking **Systems Summary** in the left-hand window will display the system information of the computer. These details include the name of the operating system being used, the system type and model and also the available memory.

T **A** **S** **K**	1.	View the system information.
	2.	Click on the cross in the top right hand corner to close the **System Information** screen.

The Taskbar And Start Button

You can use the **Taskbar** and **Start** button (as shown in Fig 7) to navigate easily through applications, documents etc.

Both features are always available on your **Desktop**, no matter how many documents you have open.

Taskbar

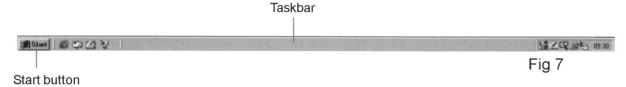

Fig 7

Start button

Depending on how your computer is set up, your **Start** menu may look slightly different from Fig 8.

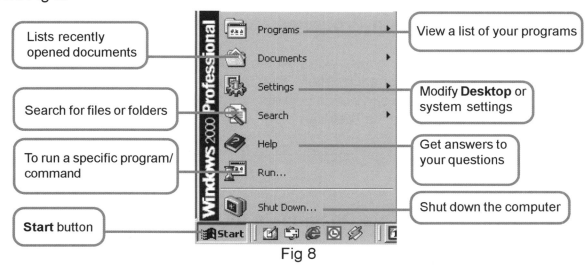

Lists recently opened documents

View a list of your programs

Search for files or folders

Modify **Desktop** or system settings

To run a specific program/ command

Get answers to your questions

Shut down the computer

Start button

Fig 8

By using the **Start** button, you can accomplish many tasks. You can start programs, open documents, customise your system, get help and more. Some commands on the **Start** menu have right-facing arrows. By placing your pointer over an item with an arrow, a secondary menu appears.

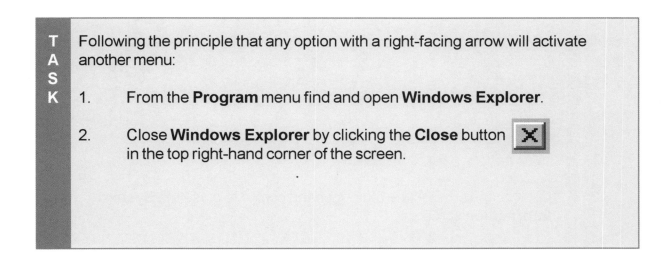

T A S K

Following the principle that any option with a right-facing arrow will activate another menu:

1. From the **Program** menu find and open **Windows Explorer**.

2. Close **Windows Explorer** by clicking the **Close** button in the top right-hand corner of the screen.

Settings

Access all your computer's **Desktop** and system settings by using the **Settings** option from the **Start** button.

Here you have access to the **Control Panel**, **Printers**, **Network and Dial-up Connections** and the **Taskbar & Start Menu**.

Click **Start**, **Settings**, **Control Panel** to activate the **Control Panel** window.

You have access to all the system properties of the computer, such as Internet options, mouse control, date and time etc.

Windows

How To Switch Between Programs (Applications)

Each application that is opened is placed on the **Desktop** and you can have multiple applications stacked on top of each other. The **Taskbar** displays the applications that have been opened. The user can switch between the application windows (see Fig 9) by clicking the relevant button on the **Taskbar**.

Fig 9

Switch Between Separate Documents In The Same Application

It is also possible to switch between documents in the same application by using a series of keys or 'quick keys' from the keyboard. Press and hold the **Ctrl** key and then press the **F6** key. This will allow you to switch between the active documents.

Scale An Application Window

Each application window has a set of scaling buttons and these are found in the top right-hand corner of your screen (see Fig 10).

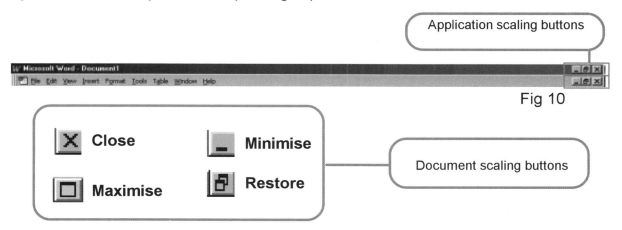

Fig 10

Close

Minimise

Maximise

Restore

Application scaling buttons

Document scaling buttons

Click the document **Minimise** button to collapse the document onto the **Taskbar** at the bottom of the screen (your work will not be lost). Click on the collapsed document on the **Taskbar** to view the document the way it was before being minimised.

Click the **Restore** button on the document window to reduce the size of the document, so that other documents behind the current application can be viewed (Fig 11). This feature is especially useful if you wish to copy data from one application to another.

Note that the **Restore** button is no longer available; in its place is now a **Maximise** button.

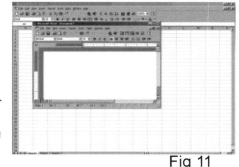

Fig 11

Click the **Maximise** button to expand the document so that it fills the application window.

Click the application **Minimise** button to collapse the application onto the **Taskbar** so that other open applications or the **Desktop** can be viewed without having to close the application. Click on the application button on the **Taskbar** to view the application.

Close buttons will close the document or application.

T A S K		
	1.	Practise switching between the application windows using the **Taskbar**.
	2.	Practise minimising, maximising and restoring the document and application windows.
	3.	Open two documents within the same software application and practise switching between them both.
	4.	Without saving any documents, close all document and application windows.

Resize An Application Window

Once the application window has been 'restored' the window may require resizing so that the data contained in more than one application can be viewed.

Click on the application **Restore** button.

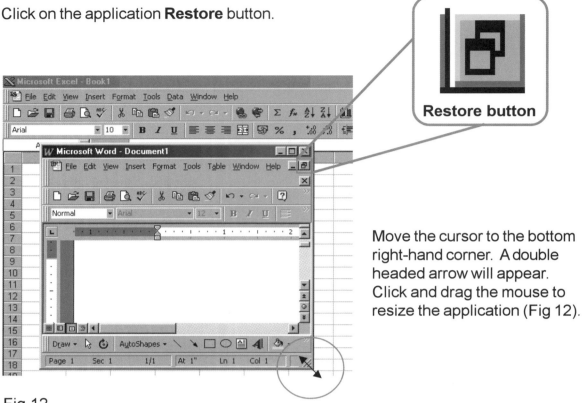

Restore button

Move the cursor to the bottom right-hand corner. A double headed arrow will appear. Click and drag the mouse to resize the application (Fig 12).

Fig 12

The application can also be resized by moving the cursor to one of the four sides of the window. A double-headed arrow will appear. Click and drag the mouse to resize the application (Fig 13).

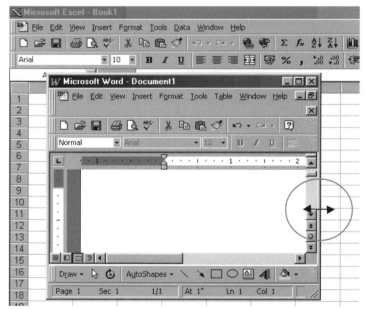

Fig 13

T A S K	1.	Open the Word application by clicking Start/Programs/Microsoft Word.
	2.	Practise resizing the application windows.
	3.	Close the Word application by clicking on the close button.

Move An Application Window

An application window can only be moved when it has been 'restored'. Moving an application window allows the user to view the contents of the other application.

To move the application window, move the mouse pointer (sometimes known as the cursor) to the **Title Bar**, click and hold the left mouse button and drag to the new position. The outline border displays where you will be moving the application to (Fig 14).

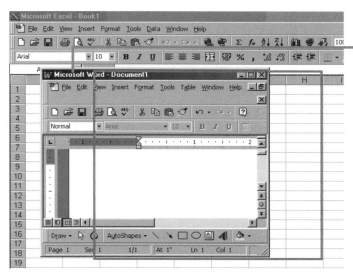

Title Bar

Once the application is in the correct position, let go of the mouse button.

Fig 14

T A S K	1.	Open the Word application.
	2.	Practise moving an application window.
	3.	Close the Word application.

Search

The **Search** menu has a number of different options, but more often then not it is used to search for misplaced files.

Select **Search**, **For Files or Folders** (Fig 15).

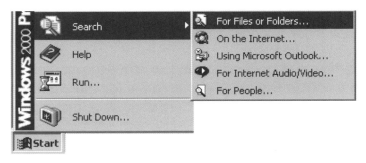

Fig 15

Fig 16

The left-hand and smaller of the two windows (Fig 16) contains the text fields that allow you to enter the criteria needed for your search.

Type the name of the file or folder in the first text field if you know it.

You can enter words that may be contained in the file you are searching for in the second text field.

From the **Look in:** drop-down menu, select the drive you would like to search. It is important to ensure the correct drive is selected. You can search all drives by selecting 'My Computer'.

You can now click on the **Search Now** button. A list of matching files will be displayed.

To refine the search further or if you don't know the filename click the **Search Options** link to activate a table containing a checkbox list of options/criteria that can be used.

It is not necessary to complete all the options; this depends on the information you have available about the file or folder to be found.

In Fig 17 the **Date** option is selected. This produces further options to refine the search. You can search for files that have been created or changed between certain dates.

Once the **Search Options** you want to search against have been selected, click the **Search Now** button.

The **Search Options** are particularly useful if you cannot remember the name of the file or folder.

Fig 17

Help!

How To Use The Help Function

Windows has an excellent system to help you when you perhaps cannot remember how to do something, or you are unsure what function the buttons (icons) undertake.

1. Click **Start**.   2. Click **Help**.

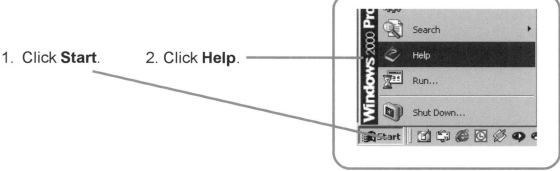

Fig 17

Click on the **Contents** tab.

Click on the book symbols to open the subjects. Click the relevant link to read the information on the subject shown in the right-hand pane. Click on the open book symbol to close the subject.

Fig 18

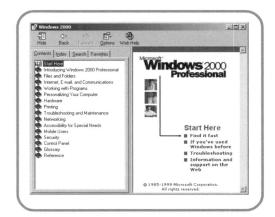

Click on the **Index** tab (Fig 19).

Type in a keyword that you wish to find. Select the heading that best matches your search from the list in the left-hand pane and click **Display**. A wider choice may be available. Click **Display** to narrow the search. The results will appear in the right-hand pane.

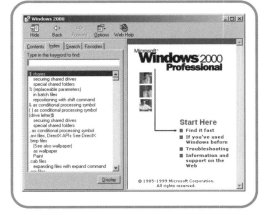

Fig 19

Click on the **Search** tab.

Type in a keyword that you wish to find. Click **List Topics**. Select the topic from the list on the left-hand side and click **Display**. The results will appear in the right-hand pane.

Fig 20

Click on the **Favorites** tab.

This sections allows you to add, and then to choose from, your favourite or most frequently used **Topics:** within Windows help categories.

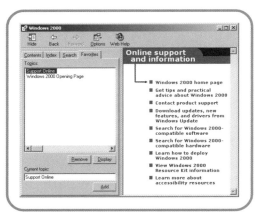

Fig 21

Run

Choosing the **Run** option from the **Start** menu is a very easy method of activating a program, folder, document or Internet web site.

Fig 22

Use the **Browse** button to locate the program or document on your computer that you would like to run. Alternatively, type the URL/web address of the site you would like to access and click **OK**.

Fig 23

T A S K

1.   Open **For Files or Folders** from the **Search** option on the **Start** menu.

2.   From the **Look in:** drop-down menu, select **Local Disk (C:)** drive.

3.   Type the word **image** in the **Search for files or folders named:** text field. The search results should be displayed in the larger window to the right.

4.   Close the **Search** facility.

5.   From the **Help** dialogue box, select the **Search** tab.

6.   In the appropriate text field, type the keyword **defrag** and click the **List Topics** button.

7.   Select **Troubleshooting and Maintenance overview** from the topics displayed in the list and click **Display** button.

8.   From the toolbar at the head of the dialogue box, click the **Options** button and select **Print**.

9.   Click **Print** from the subsequent dialogue box.

10. Close the dialogue box.

View The Desktop Configuration

Date And Time

The clock is displayed on the right-hand side of the **Taskbar.**

Fig 24

If the **Clock** is not displayed on the **Taskbar**:

Click **Start.**
Click **Settings**.
Click **Taskbar & Start Menu**.

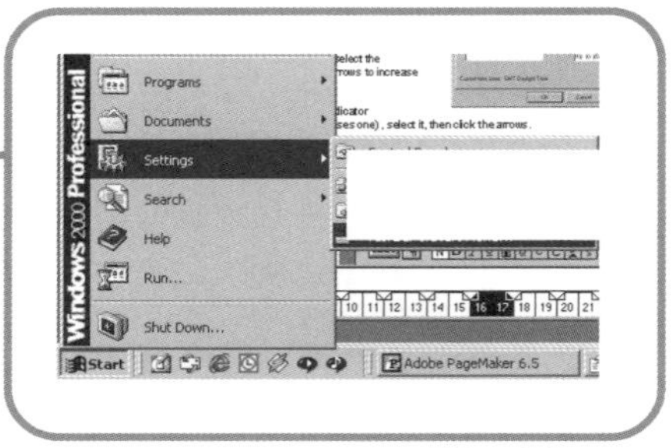

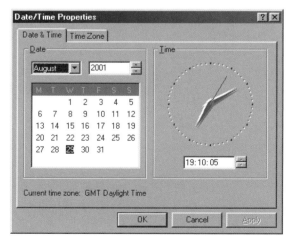

Fig 25

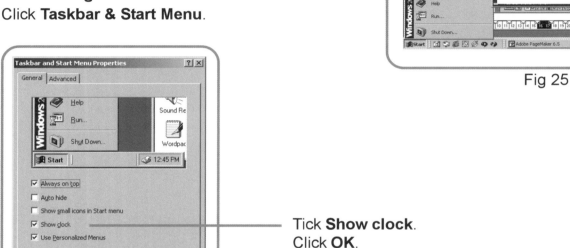

Tick **Show clock**.
Click **OK**.

Fig 26

To view the **Date/Time Properties** dialogue box, double-click the clock on the **Taskbar**. The dialogue box shown in Fig 26 will then appear.

To change the hour, select the hour on the digital clock, then click the accompanying arrows to increase or decrease the value.

To change the minutes, select the minutes, then click the arrows to increase or decrease the value.

To change the seconds, select the seconds, then click the arrows to increase or decrease the value.

Click **OK** to confirm or **Cancel** to close the dialogue box without saving changes.

Fig 27

Volume Settings

Not all computers are able to play sounds; the computer may not have a sound card inserted or speakers or headphones attached. Volume controls (Fig 28) allow you to change the settings of the sound.

Click **Start**, **Programs**, **Accessories**, **Entertainment**, **Volume Control**.

Close button

This is an example, as the controls available on your computer may vary due to the type of sound card fitted.

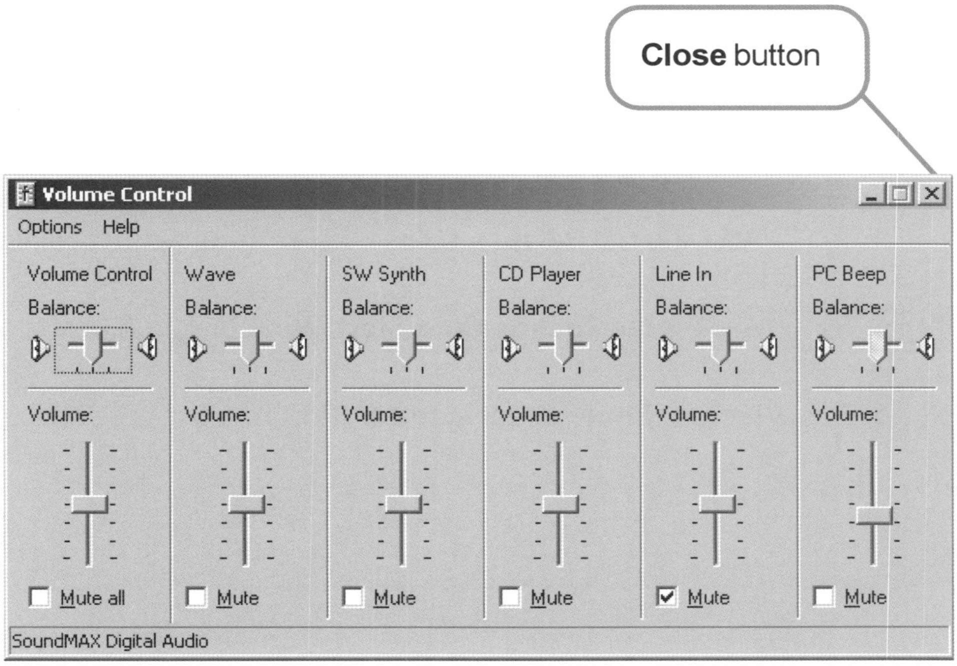

Alternatively, you can double-click on the **Volume** icon on the right-hand side of the **Taskbar**.

Fig 29

The sound can be adapted and the volume increased or decreased. Click and drag the slide up or down to increase or decrease levels. Tick the **Mute** check box if you do not wish to hear that particular sound.

Close the **Volume Control** dialogue box by clicking the **Close** button in the top right-hand corner of the screen.

TASK

You can view the volume settings on your computer, but do not change these settings unless you are instructed to do so.

CONSOLIDATION EXERCISE

1. Open the **Windows Help** dialogue box from the **Start** menu.

2. Select the **Search** tab and enter the keyword **RAM**.

3. From the **List of Topics** displayed, select and make a note of the glossary term for RAM.

4. Close the **Windows Help** dialogue box.

5. Access the **Volume Control** dialogue box.

6. Alter the CD Balance. Close the **Volume Control** dialogue box.

7. Access the **Taskbar and Start Menu** dialogue box.

8. Ensure **Show small icons** in **Start** menu is not ticked. Click **OK**.

Input Devices

Mouse/Pointer Device

A mouse (Fig 30) is a pointing device that enables you to interact with the computer. You can think of the mouse as a 'remote control'. You move the mouse across the desk, and as you do so, the mouse pointer moves in a corresponding way around the screen. Select items on the screen by pointing to them and clicking the left mouse button. The mouse normally requires a single click to 'select' or pick something, and a double click (two quick clicks of the left mouse button) to activate or open something. The mouse pointer can take on different shapes according to where and what it is positioned over.

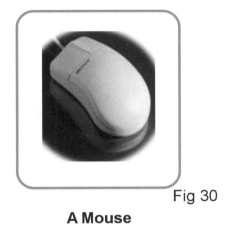

Fig 30

A Mouse

Fig 31 shows examples of the standard mouse pointers that will appear when using the mouse.

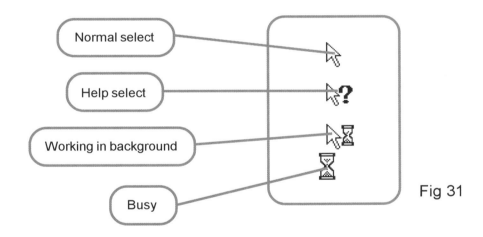

Normal select

Help select

Working in background

Busy

Fig 31

	1.	Ensure your computer is switched on.
T A S K	2.	Click **Start**, **Programs**, **Accessories**, **Games**, **Solitaire**.
	3.	Use the help menu to obtain instructions about playing the game. This will give you practise for using the mouse.
	4.	Once you have finished playing Solitaire, click **Game**, **Exit**.

Keyboard

A keyboard (Fig 32) is the most common way of entering information into the computer. The keyboard generally used is based on the QWERTY layout originally designed for the typewriter. The top row of letters begins with the letters QWERTY reading from left to right.

Fig 32

Keyboard

As well as the letter keys there are many other keys on the keyboard such as number keys, cursor control keys, function keys and editing keys. These are shown in greater detail on the next page.

T A S K	1.	View the keyboard, and locate the keys that spell out the name given for the layout originally designed for the typewriter.

Scanner

A scanner is an input device that converts printed text or images into electrical signals that the computer can understand. They are widely used to input large quantities of previously typed text. Scanners can either be flatbed (as shown in Fig 33),drum or hand-held. Flatbed scanners come in various sizes, the most common being A4. These scanners have the ability to scan a whole page of text or images at a time.

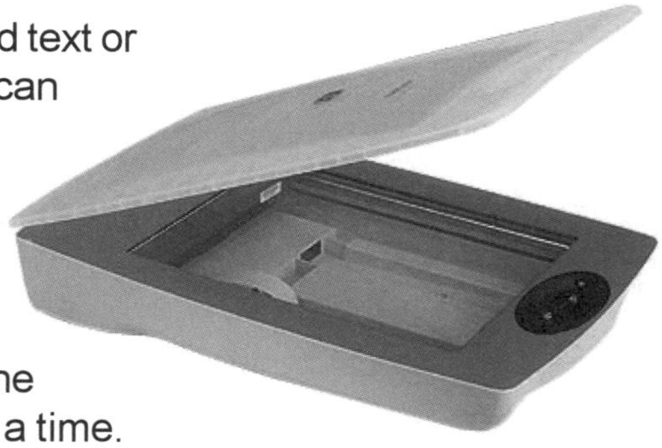

Fig 33

The Keyboard In Detail

Tab key – Used to move to preset points

Function keys – Pre-programmed to perform specific commands

Backspace key – Used to delete characters one by one backwards

Enter (or may be referred to as **Return**) – Confirms an instruction or creates a new paragraph (if in word processing application).

Caps Lock – Used to display text all in capitals

Same as other **Shift** key

Number lock, **Caps lock** and **Scroll lock** lights

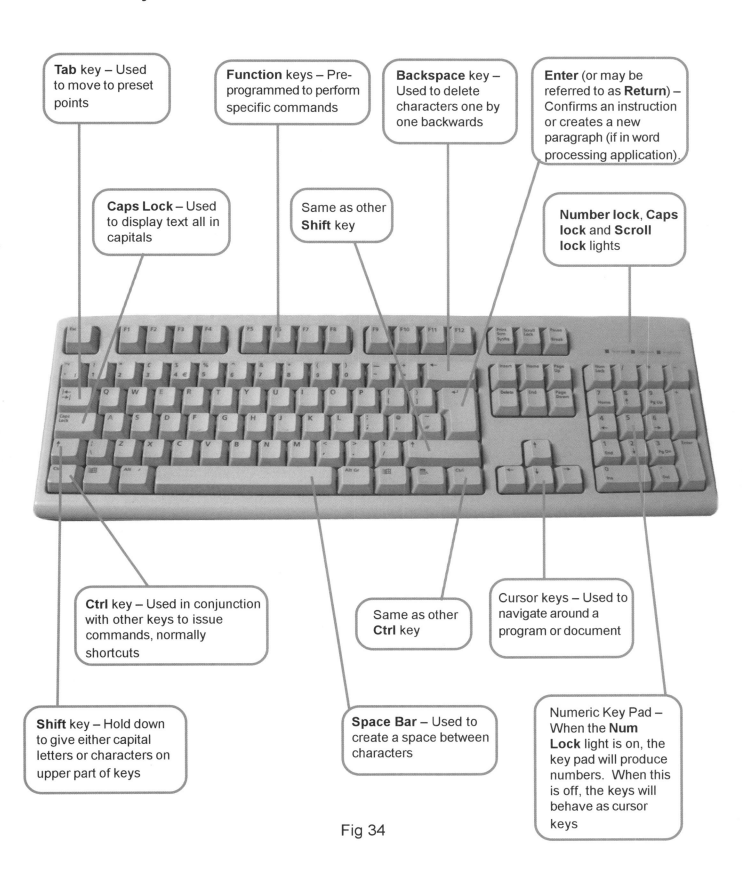

Ctrl key – Used in conjunction with other keys to issue commands, normally shortcuts

Same as other **Ctrl** key

Cursor keys – Used to navigate around a program or document

Shift key – Hold down to give either capital letters or characters on upper part of keys

Space Bar – Used to create a space between characters

Numeric Key Pad – When the **Num Lock** light is on, the key pad will produce numbers. When this is off, the keys will behave as cursor keys

Fig 34

Output Devices

Monitor/VDU (Visual Display Unit)

Monitors (Fig 35) are available in different sizes ranging from 12" to 42" in a diagonal measure. The larger the monitor, the higher the price. Common sizes of monitors are 14", 15", 17" and 21". The listed size of a monitor is measured from the inside bevelled edges of the display casing (ie the glass screen), so if considering the purchase of a monitor, be sure to ask what the viewable screen size is. This will usually be somewhat less than the stated screen size.

Generally, the smallest monitors packaged with new systems nowadays are 15". The size of monitor you require depends on two main factors: the type of activities that the computer will be used for, and the level of the end users eyesight.

Fig 35

Monitor/VDU (Visual Display Unit)

The display size of screen elements (icons, application windows etc) is determined both by monitor size and resolution. Resolution is the amount of detail that can be displayed on the screen. The higher the resolution, the sharper and smaller the graphics on screen will be. So although using a high resolution will give you sharper, clearer images and more space on your desktop or application, the icons and tools may be difficult to see depending on your eyesight, because they will be relatively small.

On the other hand, using on a low resolution will make the icons etc bigger and easier to see, but will cut down how much of an application or document window you can see at one time, causing the need for scroll bars. Low resolutions can make the screen cluttered, with large chunky graphics taking up a lot of screen space.

Experimenting with different resolutions will allow you to find the setting that best suits your monitor, software and eyesight. The most common resolutions used for web pages, games and applications are 800 x 600 and 1024 x 768.

See the table below for some resolution examples, eg 640 (screen width) x 480 (screen height). These are examples only as different resolutions can be set on most monitors, depending on your computers hardware.

Screen resolution	Recommended monitor size
640 x 480	14"
800 x 600	15"
1024 x 768	17"
1280 x 1024	21"

Pixel

While looking at the **Display Properties** settings on the next page, the term 'pixel' will be used on occasion to describe the various **Desktop** settings.

The following attempts to describe these terms and how they are used in explaining the different **Desktop** settings.

A pixel (a word invented from 'picture element') is a single point on a computer display or in a computer image.

The physical size of a pixel depends on how you've set the resolution (we will be having a look at image resolution next) for the display screen.

Screen image sharpness is sometimes expressed as dots per inch (dpi). In this usage, the term *dot* means pixel. Dots per inch are determined by both the physical screen size and the resolution setting.

Setting the screen area (Fig 36) from 800 by 600 pixels per horizontal and vertical line to 640 by 480 means fewer dots per inch (or fewer pixels per inch) on the screen and an image that is less sharp. Therefore it will have a lower resolution.

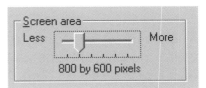

Fig 36

Quite simply, the more pixels an image contains, the higher its resolution.

Fig 37 shows a computer icon with original dimensions of 32 by 32 pixels. The larger image shows the icon zoomed to 500% so that you can clearly see the individual pixels in the image.

A single pixel is indicated by a small square outline in the upper right-hand corner.

As you can clearly see, the original image contains a greater number of pixels per inch, or dpi, than the larger image. The smaller and better quality image therefore has a higher resolution.

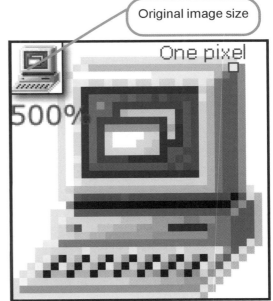

Original image size

One pixel

500%

Fig 37

Resolution

Resolution applies to both graphics designed for print (typically high resolution) or graphics created for the Web (low resolution). Choosing the correct resolution usually ends up being a trade off between image quality and file size. For graphics displayed on the web, it is better to keep the file size small so that download time won't be too long. Graphics for the web are generally made to be 72dpi (low resolution). Graphics for print don't have the same restrictions on file size and are therefore produced using resolutions up to 2450dpi (high resolution) subsequently making files that are large and require more storage space.

Display Properties

You can personalise your computer's **Desktop** using the options available on the **Display Properties** dialogue box (Fig 38). **This section is for information only.**

Access the **Display Properties** dialogue box, click on **Start**, **Settings**, **Control Panel**.

Double-click on the **Display** icon.

Alternatively you can right-click on a blank ara of the **Desktop** and select **Properties** from the pop-up menu.

Desktop Display Options

It is possible for you to personalise your computer's **Desktop**.

Background

The **Desktop** wallpaper sits in the background whilst you work unhampered in the foreground. It is visible when all applications have been minimised or closed. The **Desktop** wallpaper can be chosen from a limited set that have been installed during Windows Setup. Graphic files (pictures, photos etc) can be added to the default wallpaper list. This enables you to add pictures of friends, family, pets or vacations etc.

Fig 38

To set the **Background**, access the **Display Properties** within the **Control Panel**, or right-click on the **Desktop** and select **Properties** (Fig 39).

Fig 39

Click the **Background** tab (Fig 40) and, using the **Scroll Bar**, click on the items from the window below to select from the available backgrounds.

The item selected should be displayed in the monitor above. Use the picture display menu to **Centre**, **Tile** or **Stretch** the item.

Click the **Apply** button once you've decided upon a selection.

Finally, click **OK** to accept the image for the background.

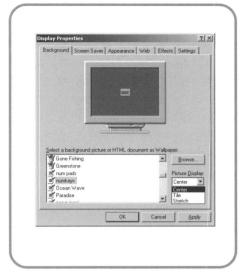

Fig 40

T A S K	1.	From the **Desktop**, access the **Properties** dialogue box.
	2.	Make a note of the current background settings.
	3.	Choose from a number of different options by using the **Apply** button; also use the **Picture Display** menu.
	4.	Click **OK** once you've decided upon a background.
	5.	Return to the **Properties** dialogue box and reset the original background.

Before continuing please ensure that the original background has been reset

---

Screen Saver

Screen savers were originally designed to protect computer monitors from phosphor burn-in.

Early monitors, particularly monochrome ones, had problems when the same image was displayed for a long time. The phosphor, used to make up the pixels in the display, would glow at a constant rate for such a long period of time that it would eventually discolour the glass surface of the monitor. Advances in display technology and the advent of energy-saver monitors have virtually eliminated the need for screen savers. We still use them as they can be fun, and also because they can help to stop others from looking at our documents if we leave the computer for a period of time.

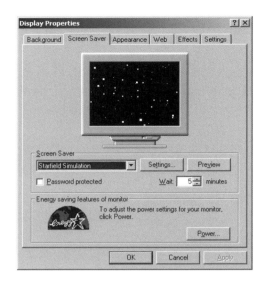

Fig 41

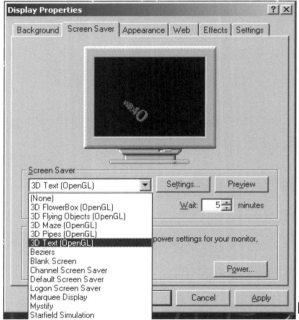

Fig 42

Choosing the **Screen Saver** tab from the **Display Properties** dialogue box will activate the window shown in Fig 41.

Click the drop-down arrow to activate the **Screen Saver** menu, from which you can select from a number of screen savers (Fig 42).

The selected screen saver will then be displayed on the above monitor. Choose from any number of options to see the various effects.

T A S K	1.	From the **Control Panel**, find and open the **Display** icon.
	2.	Click on the **Screen Saver** option and change the wait time to three minutes. Click **OK**. Close the **Control Panel**.
	3.	Using the **Start** menu select **Settings, Taskbar & Start Menu**.
	4.	From the dialogue box, ensure that all the check boxes other than **Auto hide** are ticked.
	5.	Click **Apply, OK**.
	6.	Access the **Taskbar & Start Menu** and uncheck **Show small icons in Start menu**. Click **Apply, OK**.

Screen savers are activated when your computer is left inactive for a period of time. The length of time (measured in minutes) is determined by the figure in the **Wait:** field (Fig 43). When the computer is left unused for this period of time, the screen saver will become activated.

Fig 43

Clicking the **Settings** button will provide a variety of different options that will enable you to alter the effects of the screen saver. In order to see the screen saver you have chosen without having to wait, click the **Preview** button to display it on your monitor.

Moving your mouse will close the preview and return you to the **Display Properties** dialogue box.

T A S K	1.	Make a note of your current screen saver.
	2.	Choose an alternative from the **Screen saver** drop-down menu.
	3.	Click the **Preview** button to display the new screen saver on your monitor.
	4.	Move or click the mouse buttons to return to the dialogue box.
	5.	Apply the original screen saver.

Before continuing please ensure that the original screen saver has been reset

Desktop Settings

The screen resolution can be altered on the **Settings** tab of the **Display Properties** (Fig 44) by clicking and dragging the slide to adjust the number of pixels in the screen area.

You are probably aware that the three primary colours are red, yellow and blue. However, in relation to TV screens and monitors, you also have primary colours of light or additive primaries. These colours are created by varying the light intensity of three basic colours (red, green and blue). The number of colours that can be displayed is called the colour depth. We traditionally work with the following degrees of colour depth:

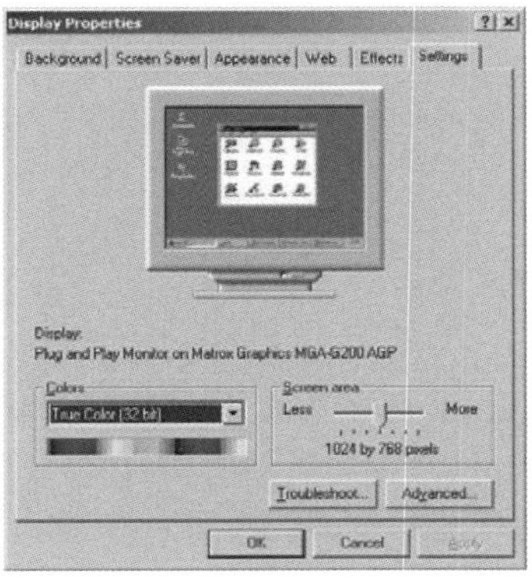

256 colour (8-bit colour)
65,536 colours (16-bit colour, also called 65k or Hi Colour).
16 million colours (24-bit colour, called True Colour).
4 billion colours (32-bit colour, called True Colour).

Fig 44

The greater the number displayed in the colour palette, the greater the depth and variety of colours displayed in your document.

NB   The colour specifications mentioned above may not be available on your machine. The specifications are dependent upon the size (memory) of the video card installed.

In the **Screen area** section (Fig 45), moving the slide handle will change the screen resolution and alter the size of the images in the monitor display above.

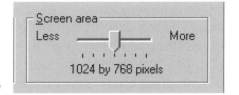

Fig 45

Once you have changed the screen area, clicking the **Apply** button will prompt the following **Display Properties** dialogue box shown in Fig 46. Click **OK** to change the computer's settings.

Fig 46

Your computer will then display the new resolution settings (Fig 48). At this stage you are given a countdown of 15 seconds in which to click **Yes** from the **Monitor Settings** dialogue box (Fig 47).

Fig 47

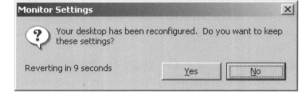

Fig 48

After 15 seconds your computer will automatically revert back to its original settings.

T A S K		
	1.	Click the **Settings** tab on the **Display Properties** dialogue box and make a note of the pixel settings in the screen area.
	2.	Change the screen area and click **Apply**.
	3.	Click **OK** from the subsequent dialogue box, then **Yes** from **Monitor Settings**.
	4.	Your screen area should now be smaller/larger.
	5.	Change the screen resolution back to its original settings.

Before continuing please ensure that the original screen area has been reset

Appearance

The colours and size of icons, toolbars, active and inactive windows can be specified here (Fig 49), enabling you to select suitable colours for your eyesight. The effect of your changes will be displayed in the appearance pane.

Click anywhere in the **Scheme:** text field to activate a menu from which you can choose the colour scheme of windows and dialogue boxes.

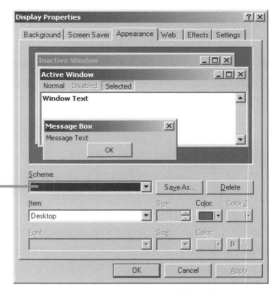

Fig 49

By selecting a colour scheme from the menu and clicking **Apply**, the colour scheme for the rest of the computer will then be altered.

Activate any software application to witness the effect of the colour scheme changes.

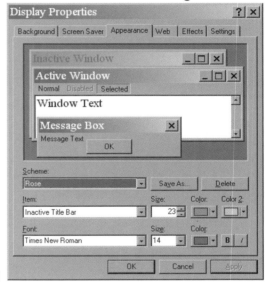

Fig 50

T A S K	1.	Change the appearance of the colour scheme on your computer by choosing an option from the **Scheme** drop-down menu.
	2.	Open any software application to see the effects of the colour scheme.
	3.	Back in the **Display Properties** dialogue box select the **Windows Standard** option from the **Scheme** drop-down menu and apply it.

Before continuing please ensure that the correct scheme has been set

Printers

Printers are output devices. They take the information you have put into the computer and recreate this on paper or card. There are several different types of printers, such as dot matrix, thermal, inkjet and laser.

A dot matrix printer (shown in Fig 51) is a low-cost printer that is an impact printer. It produces characters from patterns of dots striking a ribbon. They are used for multi-layer forms such as pay slips. However they are noisy, slow and the print quality is poor. The number of pins, typically 9, 18 or 24, determines print quality. One character is printed at a time. A dot matrix printer can be fitted with a sprocket feeder for use with continuous carbonated stationery such as invoices and pay slips.

Dot matrix printer

Fig 51

A line printer (shown in Fig 51) is a high-speed impact printer that prints one line at a time. Line printers tend to be cumbersome and noisy.

Fig 52

Line printer

A thermal printer (shown in Fig 53) is a non-impact printer that works by pushing heated pins against specially treated paper. Thermal printers are used most commonly in fax machines but are also used for labels.

Thermal printer

Fig 53

An inkjet printer (shown in Fig 54) is a non-impact printer that prints by spraying ink onto paper. Inkjet printers can spray with a resolution of 1440 dots per inch (dpi). Inkjet quality is similar to that of laser printers but the ink is less stable and needs time to dry. They are cheaper and quieter than laser printers but are not as fast. They are available in monochrome or colour.

Fig 54

A laser printer is a non-impact printer that uses a laser to produce an image on a rotating drum before transferring the entire image to paper. The drum is coated with an electrically charged film which has its charge changed from negative to positive where the laser light hits it, and this attracts the toner powder. The paper is passed over an electrically charged wire and is then pressed against the drum where the toner is transferred to the paper. Heat and pressure fuse the toner to the paper. A laser printer can have resolutions of 1200 dpi and speeds of up to 50 pages per minute.

Laser printer   Fig 52

A colour laser printer has many of the same characterisics as a laser printer. As well as the black toner cartridge it requires three additional colour cartridges which combine to match the colour printing range. A colour laser printer can print in monochrome or colour. When printing in colour the speed reduces, but the print quality is generally high. It is recommended that draft copies of a document are printed on a monochrome laser printer, and only when satisfied with the document should they be printed on a colour laser.

Fig 53

Due to the speed and high quality prints that laser printers produce they are more likely to be used in medium to large businesses with large volumes of printing.

Plotters are specialist printers used by architects, engineers and designers which produce high quality large sized prints. As the paper is much wider than A3 paper it is on a roll and prints in both monochrome and colour. They are very expensive to purchase and due to the size of the prints are expensive to run.

Speakers

Fig 56

Speakers (shown in Fig 56) are output devices that produce audio format, most commonly used for music, speech and sound effects in games. They are connected to the computer via a soundcard that digitally produces the sound patterns. Soundcards and speakers vary in quality and cost.

T A S K	1.	Ask your tutor for a set of headphones and insert them into the computer (ask your tutor for instructions).
	2.	Double-click the **My Computer** icon on the **Desktop** and select **3½ Floppy (A:)**.
	3.	Put the headphones on and double-click to select and play the **Speaker.wav** sound file.

The Personal Computer

A personal computer (shown in Fig 57) is a small, relatively inexpensive computer designed for an individual user.

There are two versions of the personal computer.

The most commonly used computer in business and industry is based on the original IBM PC. These IBM compatible machines are referred to as PCs. The company IBM developed a personal computer and released it in 1981. Since this time computer technology has increasingly developed.

The other common computer, which is used widely in publishing and design, was developed by the company Apple and is called the Macintosh, or Mac. Macs were first released in 1984 and use their own system software. More recently the 'iMac' has been released, which is a Mac designed to be more compatible with the internet.

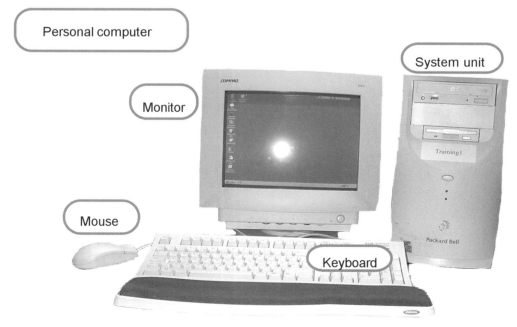

Personal computer

System unit

Monitor

Mouse

Keyboard

Fig 57

System Unit

The system unit comprises of a metal chassis and plastic outer case that make up the 'box' that contains all the components (hardware) that make the computer work.

The motherboard is mounted on to the metal chassis and all the components (disk drives, memory, CPU, sound card, graphics card etc) plug in to the motherboard.

A lot of people think that the system unit is just the outer casing, but without the hardware components it is simply an empty case. 'System Unit' is the term given to the case and components combined.

CPU

The centrepiece of the system unit is a printed circuit board, known as the motherboard, which holds the CPU chip and its support circuitry. You may also hear the motherboard referred to as the system board.

The Central Processing Unit (CPU) could be described as the brain of the computer, as this is where all the computer's instructions are processed.

The CPU receives data from all the various components of the computer such as the memory, hard disk and printer, and 'sorts out' how to perform a particular task or instruction correctly. It is the central component within the system unit that controls all others.

The speed at which your processor executes instructions is known as its' clock speed. The faster the clock speed, the more instructions the CPU can execute per second. Clock speed is expressed in either megahertz (MHz) or gigahertz (GHz). Todays' modern processors have clock speeds of about 3.0 GHz which is incredibly fast compared to earlier computers.

Hard Disk And Power Supply

Hard disks are housed within the system unit in all computers. They can vary in capacity and size. A hard disk is a fixed disk similar in size to a floppy disk but has metal magnetic plates which are encased in the drive unit.

Internal view of a hard disk drive  Fig 58

Hard disks are used to store the user programs so that they are always available. Data files are also stored on hard disks. A hard disk is fast and reliable and has a large capacity, measured in megabytes (MB) or gigabytes (GB). Hard disks vary in price according to their storage capacity and speed of access, measured in milliseconds.

Aside from the motherboard, the system unit includes disk drives (usually one or two floppy drives and one hard drive) and a power supply.

The power supply brings in power from the wall socket and supplies it to the motherboard. It also contains your computer's on/off switch and a place to attach the power cord that connects the system unit to a power outlet. The power supply unit usually contains a fan, to prevent the various chips from overheating. If your system includes an internal CD-ROM drive, modem or tape drive, it probably resides in the system unit as well.

Support Chips

The motherboard contains several other types of chips, in addition to the CPU, that help the CPU perform its job. These chips contain instructions that help the computer start up and know what hardware it contains, an example of one of these is the BIOS chip.

Expansion Boards

Most computers also contain additional circuit boards, commonly known as expansion boards or cards, which fit into slots on the motherboard. The slots themselves are known as expansion slots; think of them as parking spaces for circuit boards.

The most common expansion cards are graphic cards and sound cards, although nowadays a lot of motherboards incorporate these features 'on board' without the need for seperate expansion cards.

Bus

Finally, all motherboards contain a bus - a set of copper wires designed to carry data and instructions back and forth between various devices on the board itself.

CONSOLIDATION EXERCISE

1. From the **Desktop**, access the **Properties** dialogue box.

2. Make a note of the current background settings.

3. Choose from a number of different options by using the **Apply** button. Also use the **Picture Display** menu.

4. Click **OK** once you've decided upon a background.

5. Return to the **Properties** dialogue box and **reset** the original background.

6. Click the **Settings** tab on the **Display Properties** dialogue box and make a note of the pixel settings in the screen area.

7. Change the pixel settings and click **Apply**.

8. Click **OK** from the subsequent dialogue box, then **Yes** from **Monitor Settings**.

9. Your screen resolution should now be smaller or larger (depending on the pixel setting you chose).

10. Change the screen resolution back to its original settings.

11. Using **Appearance**, change the colour scheme on your computer by choosing an option from the **Scheme** drop-down menu.

12. Open any software application to see the effects of the colour scheme.

13. Back in the **Display Properties** dialogue box select the **Windows Standard** option from the **Scheme** drop-down menu and **Apply** it.

14. From the **Control Panel**, find and open the **Display** icon.

15. Click on the **Screen Saver** option and change the **Wait** time to three minutes.

16. Click **Taskbar & Start Menu**.

17. From the dialogue box click the **Advanced** tab.

18. Tick the check box **Display Favourites** from the **Start Settings** menu section, and then click **OK**.

    Your web page favourites should now be displayed on the **Start** menu.

19. Access the **Taskbar & Start Menu** and uncheck the display favourites option. Click **OK**.

20. On a separate sheet of paper, provide a brief description of the system unit, CPU and the hard disk. Ensure all settings have been reset to the originals.

Before continuing please ensure that all settings changed in the above Consolidation Exercise have been reset

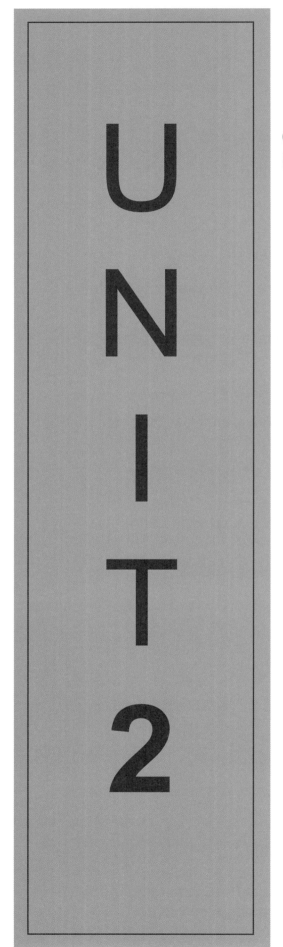

On completion of this unit you will have learnt about:

Consumables

- Printer Paper
- Paper Sizes
- Envelope Sizes
- Labels
- Cartridges/Toner

Printer Drivers

- Printer Drivers

Consumables

Printer Paper

Selecting the appropriate print material (paper, transparencies, envelopes, labels and card stock) for your printer can help you to avoid future printing problems.

The following sections contain guidelines for choosing the correct print material for your printer.

For the best print quality, using an inkjet printer, use either a matte or gloss coated inkjet paper capable of at least 720dpi printing. Before buying large quantities of paper try a sample in your printer. When loading paper, note the recommended print side on the paper package and load paper accordingly.

The following papers are not recommended for use with your printer:

- Paper with a rough or heavily textured surface.
- Erasable bond (very thin paper).
- Pre-printed papers manufactured with chemicals.

Types of paper that may contaminate the printer:

- Multiple-part forms (*carbon backed forms, ie invoice receipts*).
- Synthetic papers (*laminated paper/shopping bags*).
- Thermal papers (*for recording purposes, ie photographic paper/film*).
- Recycled paper having a weight less than 75 g/m^2 (20 lb).

If you are using a laser printer, preprinted papers such as letterheads and complementary slips must be capable of withstanding temperatures of up to 200°C (392°F) without melting or releasing hazardous emissions. Use inks that are not affected by the resin in toner or the silicone in the fuser. Inks that are oxidation-set or oil-based should meet these requirements; latex inks might not.

If in doubt, always refer to your printer instruction manual for details.

Paper Sizes

Easily the most identifiable paper size would have to be A4, as it is the standard UK size for letters and business documents. The page that you are currently reading is A4 in size and portrait in orientation.

The measurements for portrait A4 (portrait being a sheet of paper that is standing upright or vertical, like this workbook) are:

21 cm across by 29.7 cm down
or
8.16" across by 11.69" down

The table and diagram in Fig 59 and 60 illustrate a variety of commonly used paper sizes, with the measuring units being in centimetres. Dimensions for paper sizes are normally given with the width measurement first.

A6	**10.5 x 14.85**
A5	**14.85 x 21**
A4	**21 x 29.7**
A3	**29.7 x 42**
A2	**42 x 59.4**

Fig 59

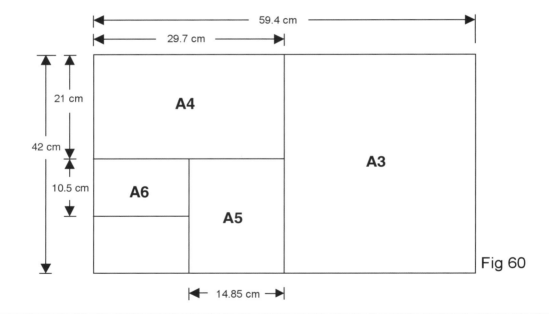

Fig 60

Close the workbook and on a separate sheet of paper attempt to answer the following.

1. What are the measurements (in inches or centimetres) of a sheet of portrait A4 paper?

2. What temperature must laser printer preprinted paper be capable of with standing, before emitting hazardous fumes?

3. What is the width of an A5 sheet of paper that is portrait in orientation?

Check your answers on page 171.

Envelope Sizes

Envelopes come in a variety of shapes and sizes, just as the items to be sent through the post can also vary tremendously. The standard-sized UK envelope, measuring 21.9 cm wide by 11 cm high, is used for sending A4 (the standard UK paper size).

The following table and diagram in Fig 61 and 62 show dimensions for the three most commonly used envelope.

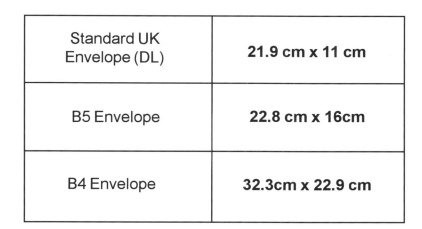

Standard UK Envelope (DL)	**21.9 cm x 11 cm**
B5 Envelope	**22.8 cm x 16cm**
B4 Envelope	**32.3cm x 22.9 cm**

Fig 61

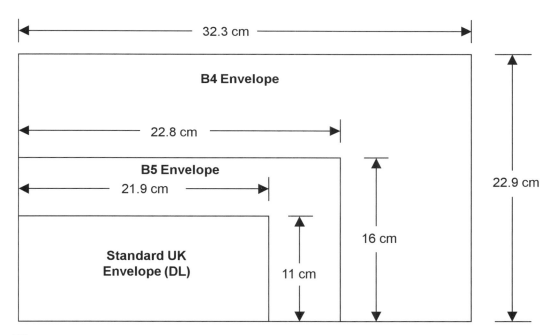

Fig 62

Labels

Just like the envelopes that they are commonly used for, labels come in a variety of different shapes and sizes.

The most widely used are self-adhesive address labels that are produced (12 - 14 labels per sheet) on A4 sheets of laser-print paper and placed in the paper tray of a printer.

The average size of an individual address label is pictured in Fig 63:

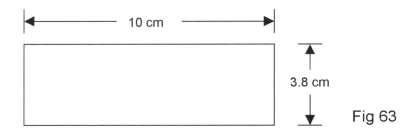

Fig 63

As well as standard sized labels, there are a large selection of blank labels for laser and inkjet printers. Label configurations are available in white matte (permanent or removable adhesive), white semi-gloss, pastel green, pastel blue, pastel pink, pastel yellow, fluorescent green, fluorescent pink, fluorescent yellow, fluorescent red, fluorescent orange and clear matte.

You can also obtain labels for compact disks and circular labels in a variety of sizes (Fig 64).

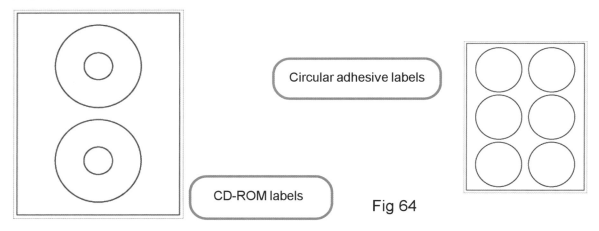

Fig 64

The chances are you can find a label to fit almost any occasion.

T A S K		
	1.	In centimetres, what is the size of a B4 envelope?
	2.	How many standard sized self-adhesive labels fit onto an A4 sheet of paper?
	3.	Name three types of computer label.

Check your answer on page 171.

Cartridges/Toner

Periodically, you will need to remove the print cartridge and clean the printer to maintain optimum print quality. You will need to have a new print cartridge available when the current one no longer prints satisfactorily.

Example Of Installing A Print/Toner Cartridge

To prepare the print/toner cartridge for printing:

•   Ensure all packaging and sealant tape have been removed.

•   Gently shake the print cartridge from side to side (indicated by the arrowheads, Fig 65) to distribute the toner evenly.

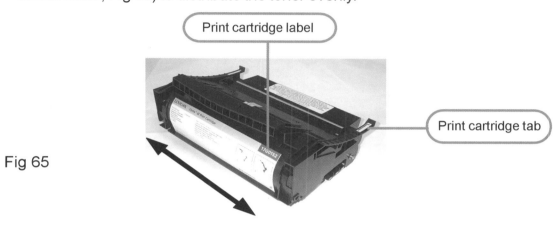

Fig 65

Inserting the print cartridge:

•   Ensure that the label on the print cartridge is facing you. Align the tabs located on each side of the print cartridge with the slots on either side of the print cartridge cradle as shown in Fig 66. Use the coloured arrows inside the printer for placement.

Fig 66

- Slide the print cartridge straight back into the printer until it snaps into place. Close the upper and lower front doors (Fig 67). If the print cartridge has not been installed correctly you cannot close the doors completely.

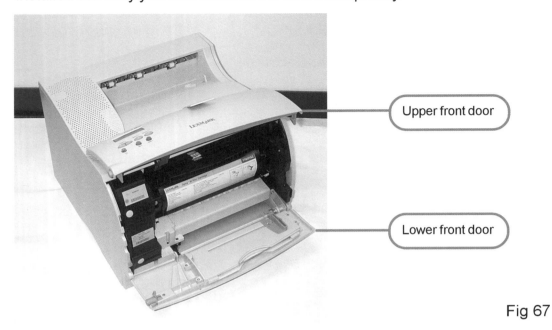

Fig 67

NB   Always ensure that you follow the cartridge installation instructions carefully.

Printer Drivers

Installing printer drivers (sometimes known as print drivers) and utilities means loading the software you need to use for your printer onto your computer.

If you purchase a computer today, the installation software will almost certainly be included on a floppy disk or CD-ROM. If your computer does not possess a CD-ROM drive, you can transfer the information from the CD onto floppy disks. Locate a computer with a CD-ROM drive, start the CD-ROM utility, and follow the instructions presented to create diskettes.

You need to follow the instructions in the manual that came with your printer in order to load the printer setup utilities.

The setup utilities let you install printer drivers and utilities to manage the printer once it is connected to your computer or network.

If your computer is networked, you may need to use standard network software to identify the printer to the LAN (Local Area Network) and to complete the setup.

C O N S O L I D A T I O N   E X E R C I S E

Close the Resource Pack and on a separate sheet of paper attempt to answer the following:

1. In centimetres, state the size of a standard UK envelope.

2. What is the size, in millimetres, of a standard sized self-adhesive label?

3. Name three types of labels and describe their uses.

4. Write the sizes (in centimetres) of sheets of A3, A4 and A5 paper that are in landscape orientation.

5. At 200ºC, what might happen to laser printer preprinted paper when it is fed through a laser printer?

6. In addition to basic copy paper for copiers and plain paper fax machines, name two further categories of print paper material.

7. More often than not, in what format will print driver utilities be supplied?

8. Before adding a new print/toner cartridge to your printer, what two points must you always ensure?

Check your answers on page 171.

On completion of this unit you will have learnt about:

Printer Setup

- Loading The Standard Input Paper Tray
- Initiate A Self-Test For A Printer
- Setting Print Quality And Selecting Transparencies
- Print Material Guidelines
- Transparencies
- Printing With Envelopes
- Cards
- Responding To Error Messages

Printer Setup

Loading The Standard Input Paper Tray

If you have a large printer with a number of different paper trays, the chances are you have a printer with a multipurpose feeder. This allows you to print a host of different types of print material, such as paper, card, transparencies, labels and envelopes.

If you are fortunate enough to have a multipurpose feeder, you may wish to print a single page print job on letterhead or other special print material you do not keep in an input tray.

For information on the types of print material that you can use with your printer, you may need to consult the instruction manual that accompanied it.

The following instructions for loading or feeding print paper into your printer tray is for information only. Always check the instruction manual that accompanies your printer.

T A S K

1. Pull the input tray out of the printer. You can pull it all the way out if you choose to.

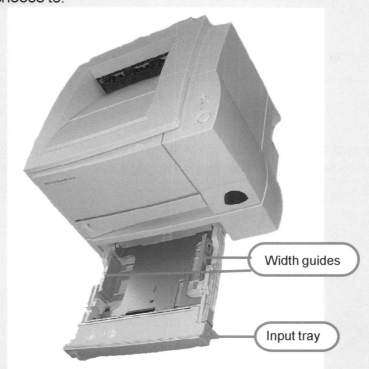

Width guides

Input tray

Fig 68

2. Place the print material against the left side of the print tray, with the recommended print side face up and the top edge going in first towards the printer.

3. Move the width guide(s) to the correct position for the size of the print material you are loading.

4. Place the print material (paper, card etc) up against the side of either width guide of the input tray and also up against the length guide.

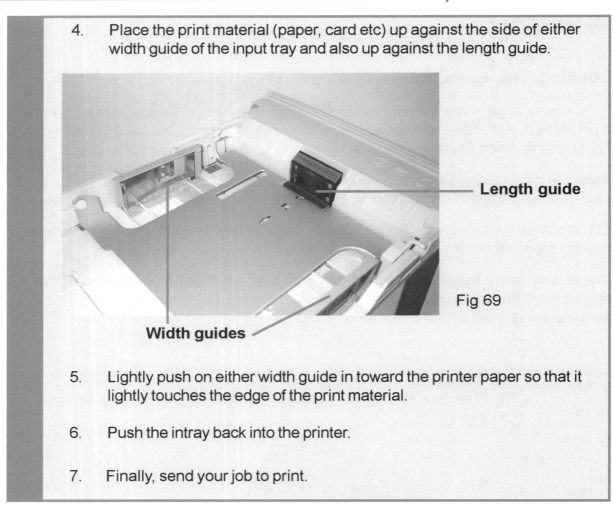

Length guide

Fig 69

Width guides

5. Lightly push on either width guide in toward the printer paper so that it lightly touches the edge of the print material.

6. Push the intray back into the printer.

7. Finally, send your job to print.

NB **Do not exceed the maximum stack height (approximately 250 sheets) usually indicated by a line or stack height limiters on the width guides of your intray (Fig 70).**

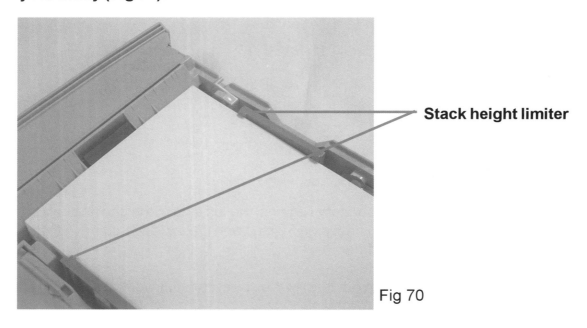

Stack height limiter

Fig 70

Initiating A Self-Test For A Printer

The procedure for initiating a self-test print can vary from one printer to the next. Follow the instructions given in order to initiate a self-test for your printer. If you encounter any difficulties consult your Tutor for assistance.

T
A
S
K

1.   Click the **Start** button on the bottom left-hand corner of your computer.

2.   From the subsequent menu select the **Settings** option and then choose **Printers** (Fig 71).

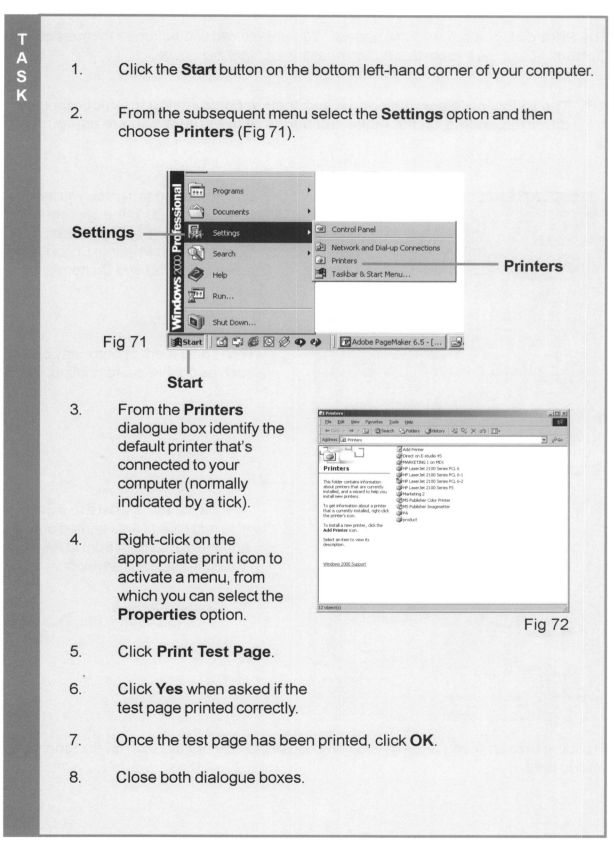

Fig 71

Settings

Printers

Start

3.   From the **Printers** dialogue box identify the default printer that's connected to your computer (normally indicated by a tick).

4.   Right-click on the appropriate print icon to activate a menu, from which you can select the **Properties** option.

Fig 72

5.   Click **Print Test Page**.

6.   Click **Yes** when asked if the test page printed correctly.

7.   Once the test page has been printed, click **OK**.

8.   Close both dialogue boxes.

Setting Print Quality And Selecting Transparencies

Assuming you're using one of the Microsoft Windows operating systems, ie Windows 95/98/2000, open any application and click on the **File** option from the **Menu Bar** to activate a subsequent menu from which you can select the **Print** option.

The **Print** dialogue box will now appear. You are offered two buttons - **Properties** and **Options**. Click the **Properties** button near the top right-hand side.

NB **The following diagrams shown and their accompanying instructions may differ depending on the make and series of the printer you are using.**

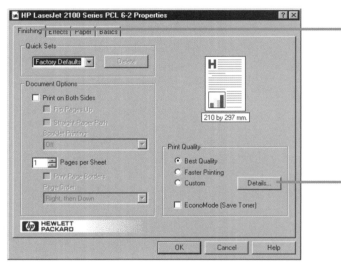

The **Finishing** tab gives you the option of selecting the appropriate **Print Quality** (Fig 72) ie Best Quality, Faster Printing, EconoMode (used for drafts) and Custom.

Other document options may be set such as double-sided printing.

Fig 72

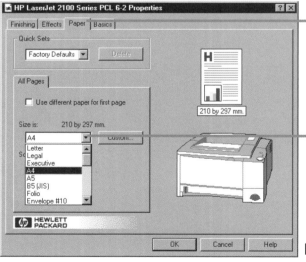

The **Paper** tab is where to select the size and type of final printed output, and the tray to print from ie A4, Transparencies or envelopes.

Fig 74

From the **Size is:** menu (Fig 74) you can choose the size or nature of the document you wish to print.

The **Basics** tab allows the number of copies to be selected and the orientation of the paper.

A preview shows the orientation and page measurements.

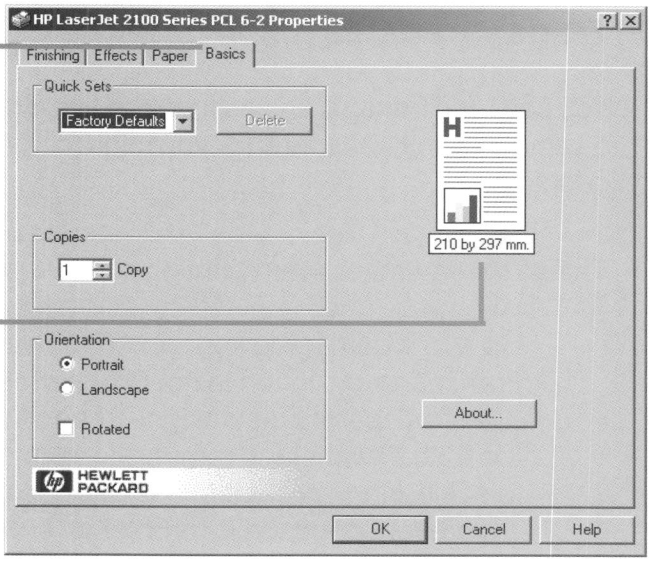

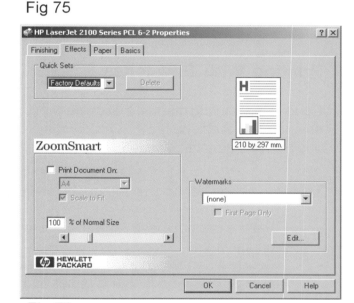

Fig 75

The **Effects** tab allows the document to be scaled up/down when printed. A watermark can also be added to the document such as 'Draft' on the first page or all pages.

The **Factory Defaults** option restores the printer's default settings.

From the **ZoomSmart** section, **Print Document On** allows you to select from a menu of sizes. Reduce or enlarge the scale of your document by using the left or right arrows.

Fig 76

Print Material Guidelines

Selecting the appropriate print material (paper, transparencies, envelopes, card etc) for your printer can help you to avoid printing problems.

NB **Instructions may vary from one printer to the next. Always refer to the information manual that accompanies your printer before attempting to print.**

T
A
S
K

1.   *Take a look at the **Properties** for the printer you have available. Make a list of the types of paper that can be printed on.*

Transparencies

You can feed transparencies from the 250-sheet input tray or the multipurpose feeder. Try a sample of any transparency you might consider using with the printer before buying large quantities.

Things to remember when printing on transparencies:

- To avoid damaging your printer be sure to check if your printer has a transparency option in the **Properties** dialogue box.
- Use transparencies designed specifically for your printer. Transparencies must be able to withstand temperatures of about 175°C (347°F) without melting, discolouring or releasing hazardous emissions.
- To prevent print quality problems, avoid getting fingerprints on the transparencies.
- Before loading transparencies, fan the stack to prevent the sheets from sticking together.

Printing With Envelopes

Consult the printing manual that came with your printer to find out the maximum number of envelopes that can be fed into your printer. Once again, try a sample of envelopes before buying large quantities to use with the printer.

Things to remember when printing with envelopes:

- Set the paper type to **Envelope**, and select the correct envelope size from the printer driver.
- For best performance and fewest paper jams use envelopes made from 75 - 105 g/m^2 (20 - 28 lb) bond paper. Do not use envelopes that:

  - have excessive curl;
  - are stuck together;
  - are damaged in any way;
  - contain windows, holes, perforations, cutouts or embossing;
  - use metal clasps, string ties or metal folding bars;
  - have postage stamps attached.

Cards

Card is single ply, and has a large array of properties, such as the orientation of paper fibres and texture, that can significantly affect the print quality. Try a sample of any card you consider using in the printer before purchasing a large quantity.

See **Paper Source Specifications** from your print manual for information on the preferred weight of print materials for your printer.

Things to remember when printing on card:

•   Be sure to set the paper type to card from the printer dialogue box.
•   Use card stock that can withstand temperatures of around 205°C (401°F) without excessive curling, wrinkling or releasing hazardous emissions.
•   Do not use preprinted card stock manufactured with chemicals that may contaminate the printer. Preprinting can introduce semi-liquids and volatile components into the printer.
•   Do not use card stock that is perforated or creased as it may cause paper jams.

Responding To Error Messages

A red circle with a cross usually indicates an error message. This means that there is a fault with one of the components that is connected to your computer.

If you encounter an **Error** dialogue box such as the example shown in Fig 77 while attempting to perform a task on your computer:

•   Carefully follow the instructions given on the dialogue box in order to rectify the problem.

•   Click the **Help** button once with the left mouse button to receive further options.

•   Report the problem to your course tutor who will be able to assist you.

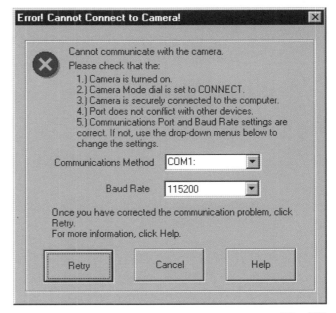

Fig 77

Internal Error/Warning Messages

An internal error may occur to your document if your computer crashes and you do not have the time to save your work. An example of an internal error is shown in Fig 78.

Fig 78

The computer may attempt to recover the document when you next open the application, but this is not guaranteed. To reduce the risk of losing valuable information, ensure that you save work at regular intervals.

CONSOLIDATION EXERCISE

1. Name two things to remember when printing with transparencies.

   Check your answers on page 171.

   Open any document and perform the following.

2. Access the **Print Properties** dialogue box and select the **Finishing** tab.

3. Print using one page per sheet and custom print quality. Click **OK**.

4. From the **Effects** tab, scale your document to 150% of its original size. Include the watermark SAMPLE. Print a single page. Click **OK** to print.

5. Choose the **Paper** tab. Select **A4** as the size and **Auto Select** as the source.

6. Click the **Basics** tab and choose the **Landscape** orientation. Print a single sheet from the document.

7. Return the document to all its original settings.

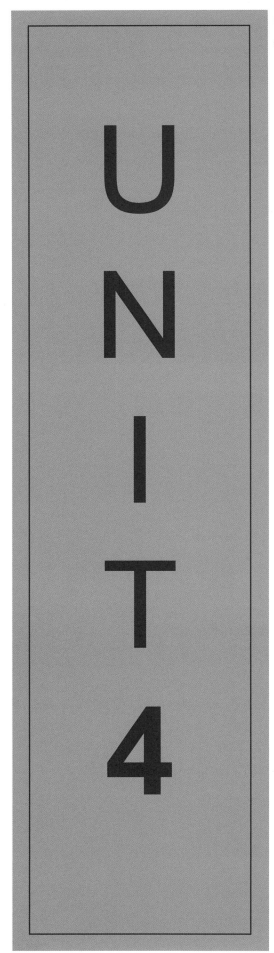

On completion of this unit you will have learnt about and practised:

File Management Systems
- Open Windows Explorer
- Windows Explorer Screen
- Explorer Toolbar
- Files And Folders (Directories)

Explorer Hierarchy
- Hierarchy Displayed In Diagram Form

File Types
- Types of File
- Office Filename Extensions
- How To Change The Views
- Changing The Appearance Of The List Of Folders And Files

Creating A New Document
- Creating A New Document
- Inserting Text Into A New Document

Saving A Document
- Saving A Document To A Floppy Disk
- Saving A Document To The Hard Disk

Editing A Document
- Editing Text In A Document
- Selecting Text In A Document
- Deleting Text In A Document
- Using The Overtype Feature
- Using The Undo Button
- Cut, Copy And Paste Within A Document
- The Clipboard
- Cut, Copy And Paste Between Documents

Closing Documents
- Closing A Word Document
- Exiting An Application (Microsoft Word 2000)

Opening Existing Documents
- Opening An Existing Document
- Print Preview A Document

Spelling And Grammar
- Checking Spelling

Sorting Files
- File Type View
- Sorting Within Details View
- Producing A Screen Print
- Gaining Access To A Shared File
- Determining Who Can Access Your File

File Management Systems

Windows 2000 can be used to organise your work into a hierarchy of files and folders that will enable you to locate and store files quickly.

Imagine trying to find the January - March 1999 gas bill if all bills are kept in the corner of your sitting room, or working in an office that kept all of its correspondence in a large cardboard box. The files you create and save can be organised like files in a filing cabinet.

Windows 2000 provides two ways of managing files and folders:

1. **Windows Explorer**   Useful for viewing the hierarchical or branching structure of the disk and its folders. Folders are opened up to reveal the sub-folders and files within.

2. **My Computer**   Useful for viewing the contents of a single folder or drive. The contents of the item selected are displayed in a new window.

Open Windows Explorer

Click **Start**
  Programs
  Accessories
  Windows Explorer

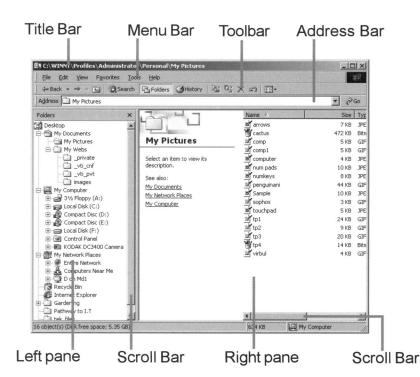

Title Bar Menu Bar Toolbar Address Bar

Fig 79

Left pane Scroll Bar Right pane Scroll Bar

Windows Explorer Screen

If you prefer to look at your files in a hierarchical structure similar to a family tree, you'll like using **Windows Explorer**. Instead of opening drives and folders in separate windows, you can browse through them in a single window. The left side of the **Windows Explorer** window contains a list of your drives and folders, and the right side displays the content of a selected folder. You can use the **View** menu to change how the files in the right pane will appear; your screen may appear different from that shown previously.

Title Bar	Displays the **Explorer** icon and the folder or drive that is being explored.
Menu Bar	Contains the main **Explorer** menus, where a selection of commands are available.
Toolbar	Displays buttons that you can select using the mouse to perform commonly needed tasks. If the **Toolbar** is not showing, click **View**, **Toolbars**, **Standard Buttons**.
Address Bar	Displays the location of a selected file. If the **Address Bar** is not showing click **View**, **Toolbars**, **Address Bar**.
Scroll Bars	Used to navigate around the panes to view all information.
Left pane	Is the part of the **Explorer Window**, which displays the drives and folders available.
Right pane	Displays the contents of the drive or folder selected in the left pane.

Explorer Toolbar

Fig 80

As with the applications you have been using before, **Explorer** has a **Toolbar** with icons (shown in Fig 80) giving shortcuts to the following tasks. Reading from left to right they are:

* **Back** moves the view through previously selected folders or drives.

* **Forward** moves the view forward through the previously selected series of folders and files after using the Back option.

* Go **Up** one folder in the hierarchy.

* **Search** for files and folders anywhere on the computer.

* **Folders** switches between the 'Windows Explorer' and 'My Computer' windows.

* **History** provide links to all the websites that have been visited on the Internet during the last three weeks.

* **Move to** allows you to cut a document from one location and paste to another.

* **Copy to** allows you to copy and paste a document from one location to another.

* **Delete** a file or folder or multiple files or folders.

* **Undo** the last action.

* Change the **Views** of the files and folders in the right pane.

Files And Folders (Directories)

Directory is another word for folder.

The files you create and save to your floppy disk can be organised like files in an office, placed into folders that are placed in drawers in a filing cabinet. The term 'file', in this context, refers to a single piece of work such as a letter or report, a spreadsheet, a drawing or a set of records from a database.

In the same way that loose papers in the traditional office are organised into folders, computer files are grouped into electronic folders. This makes it easier to find a particular piece of work. File management tasks such as copying or deleting groups of files are much simpler if organised into a neat folder (directory) structure.

Folders are displayed with the following icon:

Fig 81

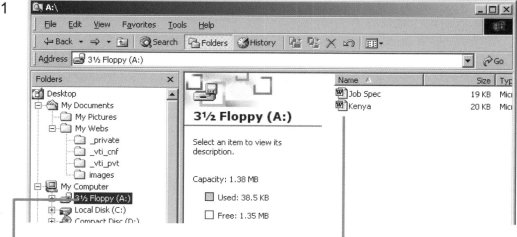

Select the drive or folder by clicking on it once.

This results in the folders and files (contents of the drive or folder selected) being displayed in the right pane.

> **T**
> **A**   1.   Select the **3½ Floppy (A:)** (floppy disk drive) to view its contents.
> **S**
> **K**

Fig 82

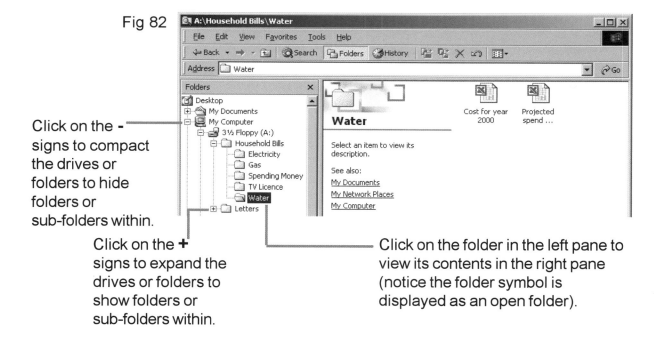

Click on the **-** signs to compact the drives or folders to hide folders or sub-folders within.

Click on the **+** signs to expand the drives or folders to show folders or sub-folders within.

Click on the folder in the left pane to view its contents in the right pane (notice the folder symbol is displayed as an open folder).

A **Sub-folder** is a folder within another folder. Fig 82 shows the **Household Bills** folder containing the following sub-folders: **Electricity**, **Gas**, **Spending Money**, **TV Licence** and **Water**.

> **T**
> **A**   1.   Find and view the contents of the **Water** folder located on your floppy disk.
> **S**
> **K**

Explorer Hierarchy

Folders and sub-folders can clearly be seen in **Windows Explorer** (Fig 83) in which the branching or hierarchical structure is clearly displayed. Files are at the bottom of the organisational hierarchy, often below several tiers of folders and sub-folders:

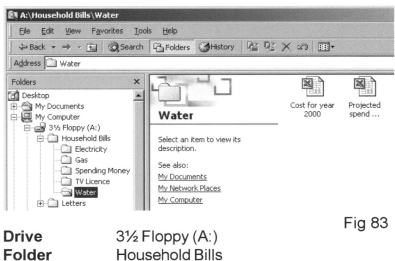

Fig 83

Drive	3½ Floppy (A:)
Folder	Household Bills
Sub-folder	Water
Files	Cost for year 2000.xls
	Projected spend for 2001.xls

NB Only contents of one folder or sub-folder can be viewed at a time. To view the contents of another folder, ie Gas, the Gas folder must be selected.

Hierarchy Displayed In Diagram Form

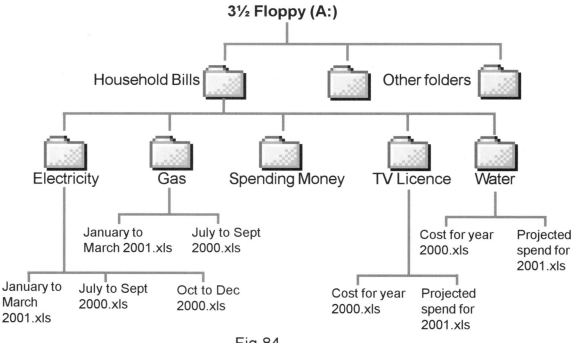

Fig 84

File Types

Types Of File

There are two main categories of file;

- Program files - which make up the software applications such as Microsoft Office and Windows 2000 itself. You should not attempt to modify or move these files. Program files have a .exe extension.

- Data files - which cover everything you produce, ranging from word processing documents, database and spreadsheet files to pictures and music. They are all referred to as files.

The most widely used types of data file are created by saving in one of the applications, such as Word. When this is done, an icon is attached to the file name to indicate the type of file. Examples are shown in Fig 85:

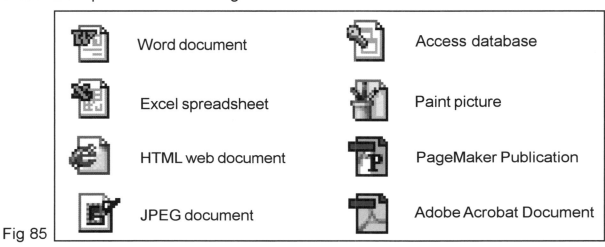

Word document	Access database
Excel spreadsheet	Paint picture
HTML web document	PageMaker Publication
JPEG document	Adobe Acrobat Document

Fig 85

Most of the files will be either text, graphic, audio or video files. Some may be compressed, others not. The most common compressed files are those with extensions like .zip, .sit and .tar. These extensions represent popular compression formats for the PC, Macintosh, and Unix. They may be single files or groups of files that have been bundled together into a single archive. An archive file can contain video or graphics files, and often contains software programs with related documentation. Occasionally you may encounter files with multiple extensions like .tar.gz, which usually means more than one type of software was used to compile and compress the file.

The following are some popular examples of file types and their headings.

Plain Text Files

- .txt The simplest and most common text file type.

- .html/.htm The language in which web documents are authored requires a web browser, such as Navigator or Internet Explorer, for viewing.

Formatted Documents

- .doc A common PC format for files created using Microsoft Word.

- .pdf Portable Document Format, a proprietary format developed by Adobe Systems, Inc. that allows formatted documents to be transferred over the Internet so that they look the same on any computer.

  This file type requires the Adobe Acrobat Reader to view files, which can be downloaded from the Adobe website.

- .ps A PostScript file. PostScript files are essentially unreadable except by a Postscript printer or with the help of an on-screen viewer.

Compressed And Encoded Files

- .exe A DOS or Windows program (executable file) or a self-extracting file. If this is an executable (self-extracting) file, then it can usually be launched by double-clicking.

- .sea A Macintosh self-extracting archive file. An archive file is usually a collection of files that have been combined into one to make it easy to download. Because the archive is self-extracting, you don't need any special application or utility to launch it. You simply click on the icon from the Macintosh **Desktop** and it decompresses and unbundles the files.

- .tar/.tar.gz/.tar.Z/.tgz A Unix archiving scheme that is also available for PCs. Tar, which is short for Tape ARchive, can archive files but not compress them, so .tar files are often gzipped, which is why you might occasionally encounter the file extension .tar.gz To download and use .tar files on a Mac, you use a program called Tar. For Windows you can use WinZIP to view and extract archive files.

- .zip A common compression standard for DOS and Windows that uses a DOS utility called PKZIP. These files can be decompressed on the PC with WinZIP. You can get copies for Windows 3.1 and Windows 95/98/2000 (winzipXX.exe).

Graphics Files

- .gif The most common graphics file format on the Internet, it stands for Graphics Interchange Format. If your browser does not have a built-in GIF viewer, then you can use Lview Pro (lviewpxx.zip) or PolyView (polyvxxx.zip) to view these graphics on a Windows PC. On the Mac, a shareware utility called GIF Converter can be used to view and modify GIFs.

- .jpg/jpeg/jfif A popular compression standard used for photos and still images. JPEG files can be viewed on any platform as long as you have a JPEG viewer. You can view JPEG files with most web browsers. For the Mac, use JPEGView, for the PC, you can use Lview Pro or PolyView.

- .tiff A very large, high-resolution image format. Use JPEGView for the Mac and Lview Pro or PolyView for the PC.

Sound Files

- .mp3 The most popular file format on the Web for distributing CD-quality music. A 1 MB file is equal to about one minute of music. This type of file requires an MP3 player, which is available for both Macintosh and Windows.

- .wav The native sound format for Windows. On the Mac, you can use Sound App to play .wav files. For the PC, use Windows Media Player or Goldwave to play these files. There is also a good program called Win Play that will play them, as well as other popular formats.

Video Files

- .avi The standard video format for Windows. These files need an AVI Video for Windows player (aviprox.exe) or the Windows Media Player from Microsoft.

- .mov/.movie The common format for QuickTime movies, the Macintosh native movie platform. QuickTime is also available for Windows.

- .mpg/mpeg A standard format for 'movies' on the Internet, using the MPEG compression scheme. There are a variety of MPEG Players for Windows and an MPEG FTP Site that has a large collection of MPEG player resources for all platforms (Mac, Windows, and UNIX).

T A S K

Close your Resource Pack and answer the following questions:

1. Can you name the two main categories of files?

2. Name two of the most common extensions for compression files.

3. What piece of software is required in order for you to view a **.htm** Web document?

4. **Zip/exe** and **tar** files come under what file type heading?

Check your answers on page 172

5. Open **Windows Explorer** and view the hierarchical content of the A: drive.

6. Close **Windows Explorer**.

Office Filename Extensions

When a file is created by saving in one of the applications, such as Excel, a four character extension is applied alongside the filename. On opening a file, the four character extension tells the computer which application to use to open the file.

Filename extensions consist of a full stop followed by three letters, making up the four character extension.

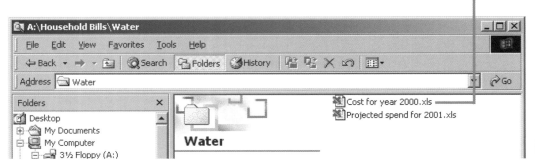

Fig 86

If the file extensions are hidden, click
Tools, **Folder Options** and the **View** tab.

> To display the file extensions, remove the tick in the box to the left of:
> **Hide file extensions for known file types**

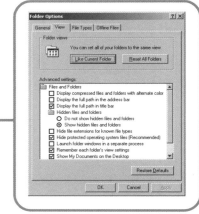

Click **OK** to accept change.

Fig 87

**NB   File extensions are usually visible, but this is not always the case.
File extensions can be hidden from view by following the above method,
but this time replacing the tick to the left of Hide file extensions for
known file types.**

Data File Extensions Common To Microsoft Office

Microsoft Word	**.doc**
Text only document	**.txt**
Rich text format	**.rtf**
Microsoft Excel	**.xls**
Microsoft Access	**.mdb**
Microsoft PowerPoint	**.ppt** or **.pps**
Microsoft Paint	**.bmp**

**T
A
S
K**

1.   View the floppy disk content and the types of file it contains.

2.   List the file type heading(s) under which each file type appears.

How To Change The Views

The appearance of **Windows Explorer** can be altered and manipulated to suit your favourite style - the concept of organising files does not change.

Working In Web Style

Work in web style if you prefer to organise and browse your computer contents using web-like options.

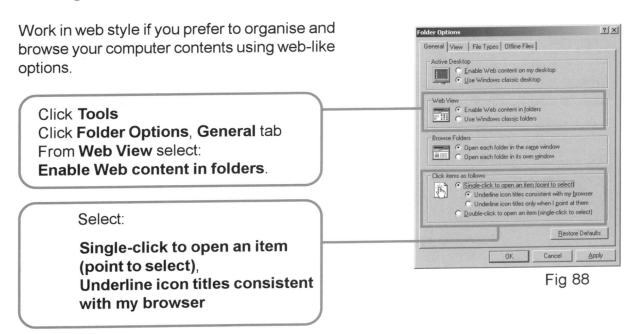

Click **Tools**
Click **Folder Options**, **General** tab
From **Web View** select:
Enable Web content in folders.

Select:

**Single-click to open an item
(point to select),
Underline icon titles consistent
with my browser**

Fig 88

Click **OK**.

To select an item, move the mouse pointer over the file or folder you wish to select. The pointer will change to a pointing hand (Fig 89). The name of the selected item is displayed on a blue background.

To open a file from **Windows Explorer**, click once.

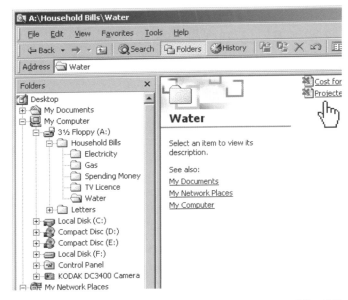

Fig 89

Working In Classic Style

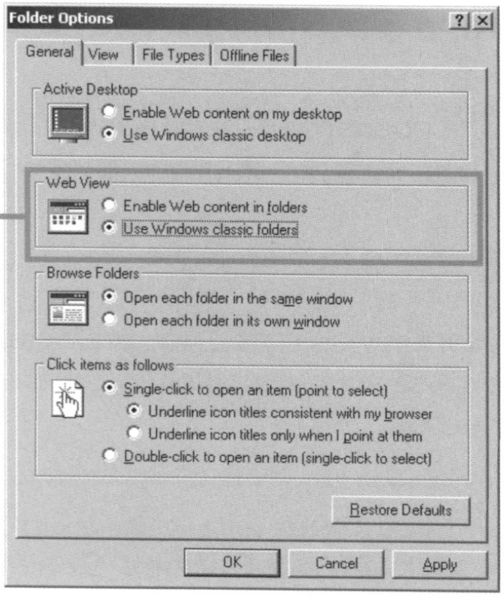

Click **Tools**.
Click **Folder Options**.
General tab.
Click **Use Windows classic folders**.

Click **OK**.

Amend the setting for selecting and opening files back to double-click as shown in Fig 91.

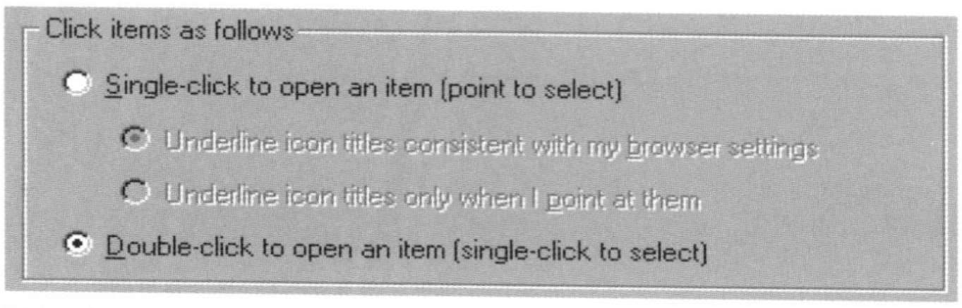

Fig 90

Fig 91

To select items, move the mouse pointer over the file or folder you wish to select and click the left mouse button once.

When selected, the item shows with a dark blue background.

To open a file from **Windows Explorer**, click to select the file and press the **Enter** key.

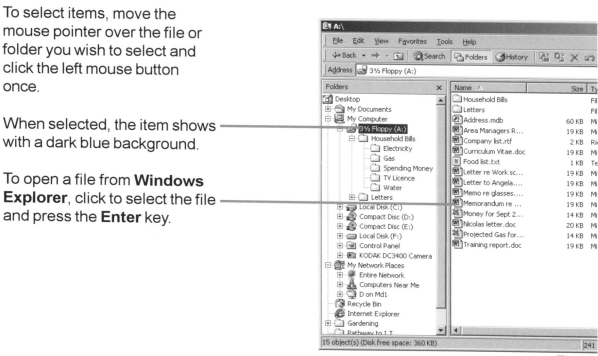

Fig 92

T A S K	1.	Change the **Windows Explorer** appearance to **Web Style**, and practise selecting files and opening folders. Close any files accidentally opened, by clicking on the cross or **Close** button in the top right-hand corner of the opened application.
	2.	Change the **Windows Explorer** appearance to **Classic Style**, and practise selecting files and opening folders. Again, close any files accidentally opened by clicking on the cross or **Close** button in the top right-hand corner of the opened application.

Changing The Appearance Of The List Of Folders And Files

Click on the drop-down arrow next to **Views**.

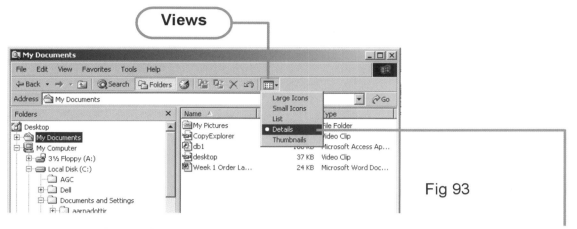

Fig 93

This displays the choices available. The option already selected is indicated with a bullet.

The files and folders are not affected in any other way except the appearance of the file icons in the right-hand pane. An example of each is illustrated in Figs 94 and 95.

Fig 94

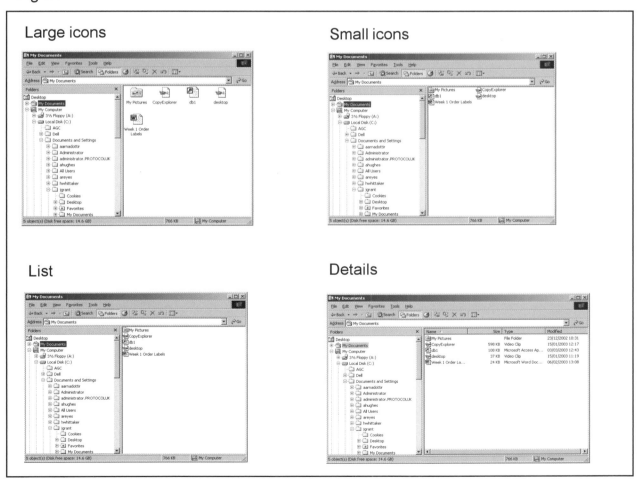

Thumbnails

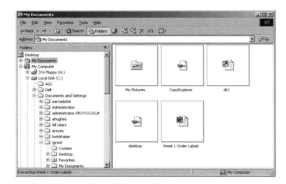

Fig 95

NB   Details displays file size, type and date last modified.

T A S K

1.   Practise switching between views.

2.   Select **Details** view before moving on.

Creating A New Document

Creating A New Document

When opening Microsoft Word 2000 it will automatically open a new blank document.

An alternative method to open a new document is to select **File**, **New** from the **Menu Bar**. This will enable you to select the type of document required. The **New** dialogue box will then appear (Fig 97).

NB **A new feature of Office 2000 is the introduction of 'chevrons' to the drop-down menus. When you select a menu item and the drop-down list appears, only certain options will appear. These are the most common options used.**

After a few seconds the full menu will appear automatically - or click the 'chevrons' displayed at the bottom to display the full menu immediately.

Fig 96

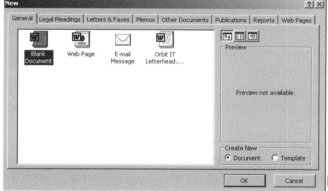

Fig 97

Inserting Text In To A New Document

To enter text into a new document, the cursor (insertion point) must be flashing in the work area. The flashing cursor determines the exact location where text will be inserted or editing actions will be carried out.

To move the cursor to another location within the document, move the mouse pointer to where you wish to start typing and click the left mouse button. Your flashing cursor will now appear in the new location ready for typing.

Entering text is normally carried out using the keyboard.

Word 2000 uses Word Wrap - there is no need to press the **Enter** key when you reach the end of the line; Word will do this for you and automatically wrap the text onto the next line. Press the **Enter** key twice (leaving one clear line) to start a new paragraph.

If mistakes are made when entering text use the **Backspace** and the **Delete** keys on the keyboard to correct.

The **Backspace** key - deletes text appearing to the left of the cursor.

The **Delete** key - deletes text appearing to the right of the cursor.

When typing a sentence and ending on a full stop or other punctuation, leave two clear spaces before typing the next sentence. One space is acceptable, however you must be consistent, ie either always leave two spaces after the full stop or always leave one space.

T A S K		
	1.	Open Microsoft Word.
	2.	Click **File**, **New** from the **Menu Bar**.
		Blank Document is automatically highlighted in the **New** dialogue box.
	3.	Click **OK** to create a new blank document.
	4.	Enter the text **The Local Wildlife Club** as a title at the top of the document.

Saving A Document

Saving A Document To A Floppy Disk

When saving a document, you are keeping it permanently and will be able to retrieve it at any time. The application allows you to give a document a name to identify it and organise your documents clearly.

To save a new document, select **File**, **Save** from the **Menu Bar** (Fig 98) and the **Save As** dialogue box will be displayed.

Fig 98

**NB   All tasks carried out using this workbook will be saved to 3½ Floppy (A:).
Always ensure you have a floppy disk in the drive before attempting to save.**

Once a document has been saved to disk, the file name will appear alongside the application name on the **Title Bar**. This is confirmation that the document has been saved correctly.

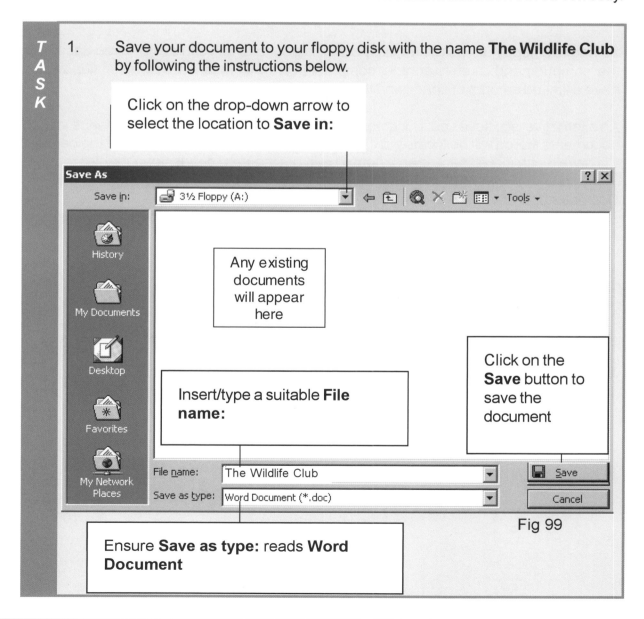

TASK

1. Save your document to your floppy disk with the name **The Wildlife Club** by following the instructions below.

Click on the drop-down arrow to select the location to **Save in:**

Any existing documents will appear here

Click on the **Save** button to save the document

Insert/type a suitable **File name:**

Ensure **Save as type:** reads **Word Document**

Fig 99

To save the document as you work, click **File**, **Save** from the **Menu Bar**. As the document has already been named and saved, no dialogue box will appear; any updates to the document will be saved. The document's name will remain the same.

Using The Save As Command

It may be necessary to make amendments to a document and keep both the original and the updated version. The **Save As** command is used for this. By opening an existing document, amending or editing it and using **File**, **Save As** from the **Menu Bar**, the document can be given a different name and both versions can be saved.

Once the **Save As** command has been used, the new document name will appear on the **Title Bar**.

Saving A Document To The Hard Disk

A similar procedure is used to save documents to the hard disk of the computer. The reasons to save to floppy disk or hard disk should be taken into consideration.

Saving to a floppy disk is useful, as the disk is portable, ie it can be removed easily from the computer and taken to another computer in another location. However, floppy disks have a limited amount of space and therefore can fill up quite quickly.

An alternative is to save your documents to the computer's hard disk. This means that any documents stored will be located in the computer. This can be beneficial, as the hard disk will have much more space than a floppy disk, but the hard disk is not portable.

Computer disk drives are assigned a letter by the computer: the floppy disk drive is known as the A: drive and the hard disk is usually known as the C: drive. However, this can vary depending on the computer system you are using.

> You are not required to complete this - **it is for information only**.

To save to the hard disk, click **File**, **Save** or **File**, **Save As** and select the location using the drop-down arrow as before (Fig 100).

If you are saving to folders, locate the required folder and when it appears in the **Save in** box click **Save**.

Fig 100

Editing A Document

Editing Text In A Document

To edit text in a document is to amend or change it. This can be changing the order of text, replacing text or adding text. You may also need to format the text so that it appears differently.

To edit a piece of text you must place the cursor at the correct position where the editing is to take place. For example, the following sentences have been entered into a new Word document. The document is to be edited to ensure the text is correct:

> I am writing regarding my new acccount details. I would like to discuss the possibility of setting up new direct debit instructions on the account.

One of the sentences contains a spelling error. To edit, the cursor is placed in between one of the letter 'c's in the word 'account' in the first sentence. The cursor will flash to indicate its position:

> acc|count

Edit the word by using the **Backspace** or **Delete** keys on the keyboard.

Selecting Text In A Document

When working with text in a document, many tasks will require the text being selected (or highlighted) first. This is so that Word 2000 knows which piece of text to perform an action on.

For example, to enhance a piece of text, such as make bold or underline, select the text first and then click on the bold or underline button on the Toolbar.

The selected or highlighted text in this example appears in the dark shading:

> Your name here
>
> Over the past year The Wildlife Club has been visiting Zoos and National Parks. Some are involved in the conservation of animals.

When the mouse is moved over text in a document it will change in shape - instead of a pointer it will change to an I-beam that looks like this: I

To Select Text

Point at the start of the text, press and hold the left mouse button, and drag the highlight over the text. Once the required text has been selected, release the mouse button.

or

Click at the start of the required text, press and hold the **Shift** key, and use the arrow keys to select the required text. Once the required text has been selected, release the keys.

To select:

One word	-	Double-click with the mouse anywhere on the word.
One sentence	-	Press and hold the **Ctrl** button on the keyboard and click anywhere in the sentence.
One paragraph	-	Triple-click (three clicks on the mouse button) anywhere in the paragraph.

To cancel a selection, click anywhere in the work area of the Word window.

Deleting Text In A Document

When editing a document it may be necessary to delete selected parts of the text. This could be characters, words, sentences, paragraphs or complete sections of text.

Use the selecting or highlighting procedure to indicate which piece of text is to be deleted.

To delete, either use the **Delete** key or the **Backspace** key on the keyboard.

To delete text and replace it with new text, select/highlight it and type. The original text will be replaced as you type.

Using The Overtype Feature

If a large amount of text is to be replaced with new text in a document, you may find that you need to use the Overtype feature in Word. When this is activated, the cursor can be placed at the beginning of a piece of text and instead of deleting first, you can type over the existing text, replacing it as you type.

To activate the Overtype feature locate the **Status Bar** at the bottom of the Word window. You will see a button stating the letters **OVR.** OVR

If this is not activated it will appear 'greyed out' or 'faded'.

To activate it, double-click on it and it will appear in black text (as above).

When editing any existing text, you will be typing 'over' the existing text.

Take care to ensure this feature is 'inactivated' when not required.

Using The Undo Button

If you make a mistake at any time, use the **Undo** button on the **Standard** toolbar to undo your last action.

Click on the **Undo** button.

To select a previous action to **Undo**, click on the drop-down arrow to view the actions you have carried out (Fig 101).

Fig 101

T A S K

1. Add the following text to your document on a clear new line below the title:

> We are delighted to announce that a large donation has been given to our club by Mr. Ramsay of Bellings Construction Limited. We would like to thank him very much.

(Your line endings may differ from those above.)

2. Save the changes to the document.

3. Amend the word **delighted** to **pleased**.

4. 'Mr. Ramsay' is in fact 'Mrs. Ramsay'. Edit the document as necessary.

5. Save the changes to the document.

6. 'Bellings Construction' should be 'Belling Construction'. Edit as necessary.

7. Use the overtype facility to change the word **him** to **her** in the last sentence.

8. Save the changes to the document.

Cut, Copy And Paste Within A Document

Three useful tools within any of the Microsoft Office 2000 applications are **cut**, **copy** and **paste**. Within Word 2000 they are used to move and copy text within and between documents.

Cut - To move a selected piece of text from one location to another.

Copy - To duplicate a selected piece of text to create a copy.

Paste - To complete either of the above actions.

Cut, **copy** and **paste** are available on the **Standard Toolbar** located at the top of the screen and the buttons are as above.

The Standard Procedure For Cutting and Pasting or Copying and Pasting

1. Select the text.
2. Click either **Cut** (move) or **Copy** (duplicate).
3. The selected text is placed on the Clipboard (see next section).
4. Select the required location and click on **Paste**.

The **cut**, **copy** and **paste** commands are also available from the **Menu Bar** by selecting **Edit**.

The Clipboard

The Clipboard is an area of temporary memory which will hold data, whether cut or copied, for it to be pasted elsewhere.

When an item is copied, the original will stay in its original position, and a copy will be placed on the Clipboard.

The Clipboard is common to all Office applications; therefore data can be cut or copied from one document to another or from one application to another.

When a piece of data has been cut or copied to the Clipboard it will remain there until the Clipboard is full or the computer is switched off.

Cut, Copy And Paste Between Documents

To use **cut**, **copy** and **paste** between documents:

1. Open or view the document from where the text is to be cut or copied.

2. Select the text, and click on **Cut** or **Copy**.

3. Open or view the document where the text is to be pasted or copied to.

4. Position the cursor and click on **Paste**.

5. Close any active or open documents which are no longer required.

TASK

1. Use your document called **'The Wildlife Club'**. Copy the word **donation** from the first sentence and place the copy on a clear line below the first paragraph, as shown below:

    > The Wildlife Club
    >
    > We are pleased to announce that a large donation has been given to our club by Mrs. Ramsay of Belling Construction Limited. We would like to thank her very much.
    >
    > donation

2. Open a new blank document in Word and copy the text **Belling Construction Limited** into the new document.

3. Save the new document with the name **Belling** to your floppy disk.

4. Save the changes to **The Wildlife Club** document.

Closing Documents

Closing A Word Document

Once you have finished working with a document, it is important to close it and exit the application. This will eliminate any risk of your work being lost or tampered with.

> **T A S K**
>
> To close any open (active) documents, follow the next set of instructions:
>
> 1. Click **File** from the **Menu Bar**.
>
> 2. Click **Close**.
>
> This will close down the active document and not Microsoft Word 2000.
>
> 3. Close any open documents in Word.

Exiting An Application (Microsoft Word 2000)

> **T A S K**
>
> To close Microsoft Word 2000 follow the next set of instructions.
>
> 1. Click **File** from the **Menu Bar** (Fig 102).
>
> 2. Click **Exit**.
>
> Or use the **Close** button. Locate the set of buttons at the very top right corner of the Word window, to the right of the **Title Bar**. Click on the top cross to close the application.

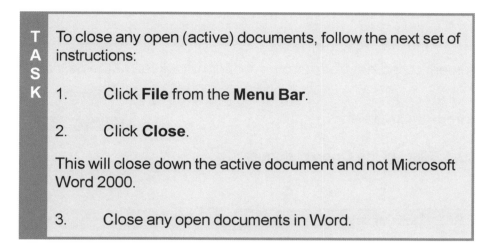

Fig 103

Fig 102

When using either of the above methods you may receive a message (Fig 104) asking if you would like to save any changes to a document (it may display the document name). If you have made any changes since the last save, ensure you select **Yes.**

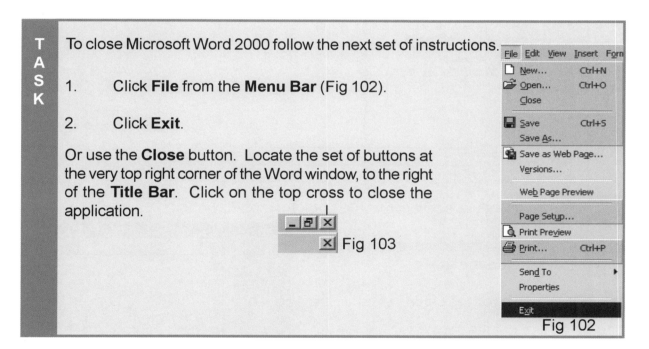

Fig 104

Opening Existing Documents

You may need to look at or amend a document that has been saved.
Before commencing this task, open Microsoft Word.

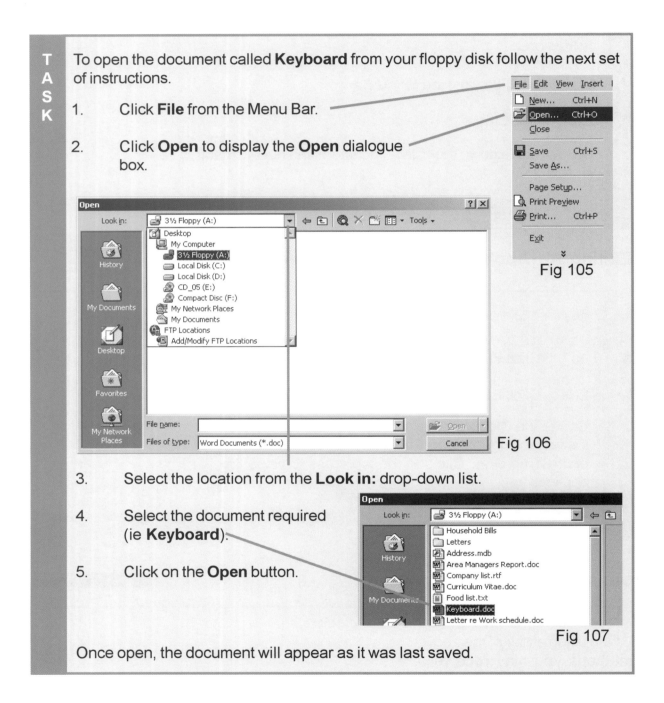

T A S K

To open the document called **Keyboard** from your floppy disk follow the next set of instructions.

1.   Click **File** from the Menu Bar.

2.   Click **Open** to display the **Open** dialogue box.

Fig 105

Fig 106

3.   Select the location from the **Look in:** drop-down list.

4.   Select the document required (ie **Keyboard**).

5.   Click on the **Open** button.

Fig 107

Once open, the document will appear as it was last saved.

Print Preview A Document

Microsoft Word 2000 has a facility called print preview. This is accessible by clicking on the **Print Preview** button on the standard toolbar or by selecting **File**, **Print Preview** from the **Menu Bar**.

The purpose of print preview is to display the document as it will look when printed. By using this feature before you print, the document can be checked for layout, orientation and margins etc. Viewing a page before printing saves wasted print ie paper and ink. Print preview is known as a **WYSIWYG** feature (**W**hat **Y**ou **S**ee **I**s **W**hat **Y**ou **G**et) - the document that you see on screen will match the printed document.

Print preview will open in its own window and has its own toolbar. The print preview toolbar is shown in Fig 108. To return to your document click on the **Close** button.

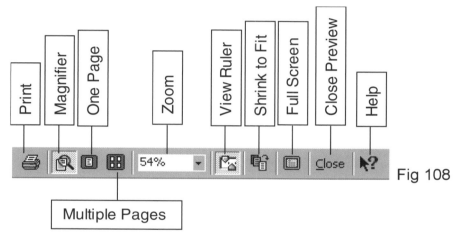

Fig 108

Multiple Pages

The Print Preview Window

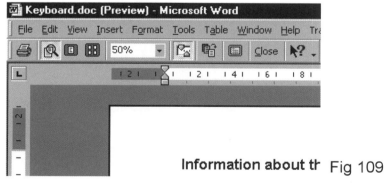

Information about th Fig 109

Notice that the document name will still appear on the title bar. However, the word 'Preview' will also appear in brackets to indicate that you are previewing the document (Fig 109). The document will appear as it will be printed on paper.

T A S K		
	1.	Preview a document that you have previously used.
	2.	Print the document.
	3.	Close the Print Preview and return to the document.
	4.	Close the document without saving any changes.

Spelling And Grammar

Checking Spelling

All word processed documents should be checked for spelling errors. This is sometimes known as proofing or proof reading. Word 2000 has a facility to do just this and checks each word in your document against a standard dictionary. If a word is unknown to the dictionary it will be 'flagged' by the appearance of a red wavy line underneath the word (if this feature is activated on your computer).

You can choose to either check the whole document or a selection which has been highlighted. If checking the whole document, ensure the cursor is at the top (beginning) of the document. The check will commence from where the cursor is positioned.

Either use the button on the **Standard** toolbar to activate the spell checker

or select **Tools**, **Spelling and Grammar** from the **Menu Bar** (Fig 110).

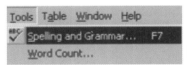 Fig 110

The **Spelling and Grammar** dialogue box shown in Fig 111 will be displayed.

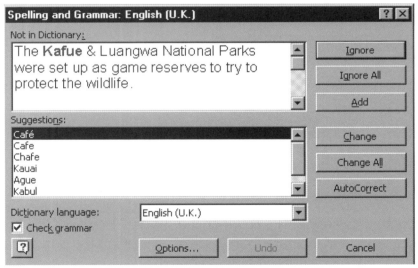 Fig 111

Notice the **Not in Dictionary** box is displaying the unrecognised word in red together with a suggestion in the box below.

The buttons on the right of the dialogue box are:

Ignore	-	Skips the highlighted word without making changes.
Ignore All	-	Skips over all occurrences of the word throughout this document only without making changes.
Add	-	Adds the highlighted word to the dictionary on the computer.
Change	-	Replaces the original word with a chosen suggestion.
Change All	-	Replaces all occurrences of the word with a chosen suggestion.
AutoCorrect	-	Adds a misspelled word and its correction to the AutoCorrect list; future misspelling of the word will be automatically corrected.

One of the above buttons must be selected before the checker can move onto the next word within the document.

The spell checker may not recognise the names of people or places. If they are used regularly, check them manually and then add to the dictionary.

Once the spell checker reaches the end of the document, it will display the message shown in Fig 112.

Click **OK**.

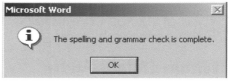

Fig 112

T **A** **S** **K**	1.	Open the document called **The Wildlife Club**.
	2.	Spell check the document and make any amendments if necessary.
	3.	Save the changes to the document.
	4.	Close the document.
	5.	Close Microsoft Word 2000.

Sorting Files

File Type View

Finding files can be made easier by sorting the files by name, size, type or date modified.

Click **View**

Click **Arrange Icons**

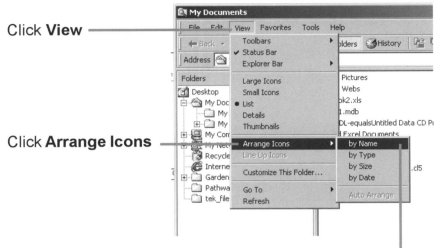

Choose the type of file-sort from the selection available.

Fig 113

Sorting Within Details View

Click on the column titles to sort the contents.

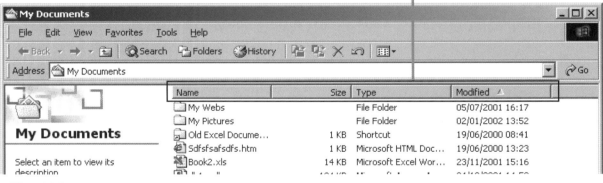

Fig 114

T A S K	1.	Using **Windows Explorer**, view a folder.
	2.	Practise sorting the contents by name, type, size and date modified. Sort by name order before continuing.

Producing A Screen Print

Fig 115

To produce a copy of everything that is displayed on the screen of your monitor (almost like a photograph or snapshot), click the **Print Screen** button in the top right area of the keyboard.

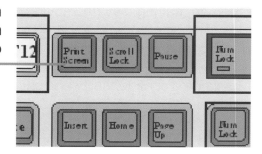

Inside the document page where you would like to insert the image click **Edit**, **Paste** or **Ctrl+V** to add the screen print image.

You can then resize, crop or move the image within the document as you see fit.

CONSOLIDATION EXERCISE

1. Using **Windows Explorer**, access and select the **3½ Floppy (A:)** (floppy disk drive) to view the files it contains.

2. Find and view and name the contents of the **Household Bills** folder located on your floppy disk.

3. Can you name two file extensions belonging to the sound file format?

4. .mpeg/.mov and .avi come under which file type heading?

5. .jpeg, .gif and. tiff files come under which file type heading?

6. View the hierarchical content of the A: drive as seen through **Explorer**. Produce a screenshot of the **Explorer** window, paste it into a Word document and produce a printout. Close **Microsoft Explorer**.

7. View the floppy disk content and name the types of file extension(s) it contains.

8. List the file type heading(s) under which each file type appears.

9. Change the **Windows Explorer** appearance to **Web Style**, and practise selecting files and opening folders. Close any files accidentally opened by clicking on the cross or **Close** button in the top right-hand corner of the opened application.

10. Change the **Windows Explorer** appearance to **Classic Style**, and practise selecting files and opening folders. Again, close any files accidentally opened by clicking on the cross or **Close** button in the top right-hand corner of the opened application.

11. Practise sorting the contents by name, type, size and date modified. Sort by name order before continuing.

Check your answers on Page 172

Gaining Access To A Shared File (Information Only)

Opening, editing, saving, moving, copying or indeed any other sort of file management is almost no different with a shared file than it is with any other. The only difference is that you need to gain access to the file first.

Maintaining confidentiality and privacy over the network is important. This can be achieved by:

• Closing down or logging off when absent from the computer.
• Not giving out your password.
• Setting user access (described below).

As part of a computer network in Windows 2000 you will be able to see all the computers that are on your network. However, this does not allow access to the drives on each computer. To access files you will need to enter your user name, followed by your password. This will need to be entered in the **Network Password** dialogue box (Fig 116) before you are allowed access.

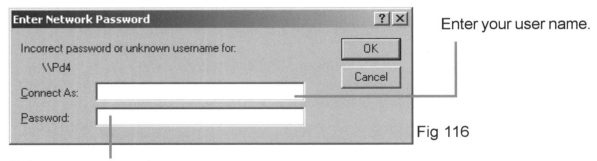

Enter your user name.

Fig 116

Enter your password.

The network will check to see if you are allowed to log on, and will then allow you access. This will be determined and set up by your network administrator.

Determining Who Can Access Your Files (Information Only)

Open the **My Computer** dialogue box on the **Desktop** and right-click the **Local Disk (C:)** (or right-click on the **C: drive** icon using **Windows Explorer**). From the pop-up menu, choose **Sharing**.

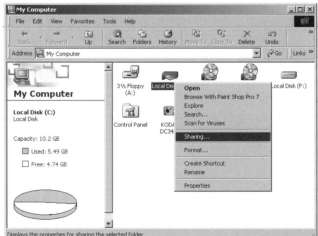

Fig 117

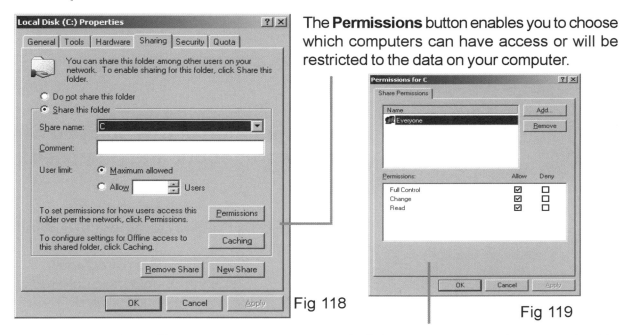

The **Permissions** button enables you to choose which computers can have access or will be restricted to the data on your computer.

Fig 118

Fig 119

The **Name** section will contain the user names of all the computers on the network with access to your computer. Use the **Add** button to select from a list of users on the network or use the **Remove** button to restrict access.

From the **Permissions** section, you can determine the degree to which users can manipulate the files on your machine.

Clicking either the **Allow** or **Deny** check boxes, you can give permission for users to have **Full Control**, the capacity to **Change**, or access to simply **Read** the information on your computer.

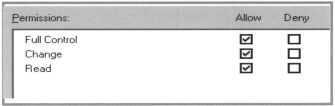

Fig 120

To see any other users on your network, you can do the following- in Windows 2000, using **Windows Explorer**, go to **My Network Places**.

It is not adviseable to share your C: drive with 'Everyone' on a network. This is mainly for allowing trusted colleagues to view and access files held on your PC. Potential dangers include files and system files being deleted, files being amended and confidential documents being accessed. The centre computers have been set up so that you do not need to use passwords to see other users - instead the machines have been configured to allow you to access the parts of the network you need to use. **Ask your tutor to show you this.**

T A S K	1.	Using the method above for your operating system, write down if there are any other users on your network.
	2.	Can you gain access to the drives or have they had permissions set to deny access?
	3.	Have a look at your C: drive. Does this have sharing allowed?

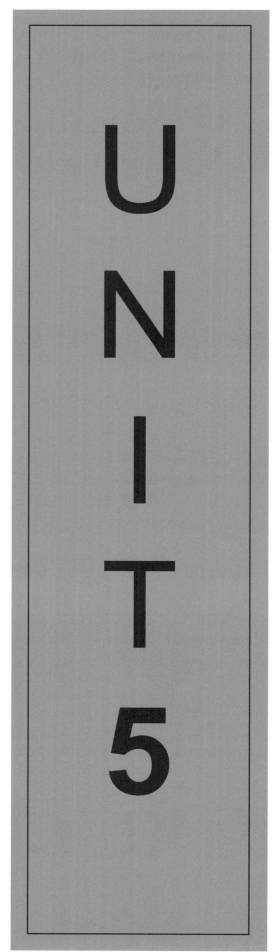

On completion of this unit you will have learnt about and practised:

- **Creating Folders (Directories) In Windows Explorer**
  - Creating Folders (Directories)
  - Creating Sub-folders (Sub-directories)
  - Moving Files And Folders
  - Copying Files And Folders
  - Multiple File Selection

- **Renaming Files And Folders**
  - Renaming Files
  - Renaming Folders
  - Deleting Files Or Folders

Creating Folders (Directories) In Windows Explorer

Creating Folders (Directories)

Directory is another word for folder. Folders can contain many files and sub-folders, and they should be given names that you will be able to recognise instantly, rather than having to open each folder and view the contents.

Highlight the **3½ Floppy (A:)** by clicking ONCE with the mouse.

Fig 121

Select **File**, **New**, **Folder**

Fig 122

A new folder icon will appear on the right-hand side of the screen, high-lighted and ready for you to type in your folder name. You do not need to delete the words 'New Folder' before entering your folder name.

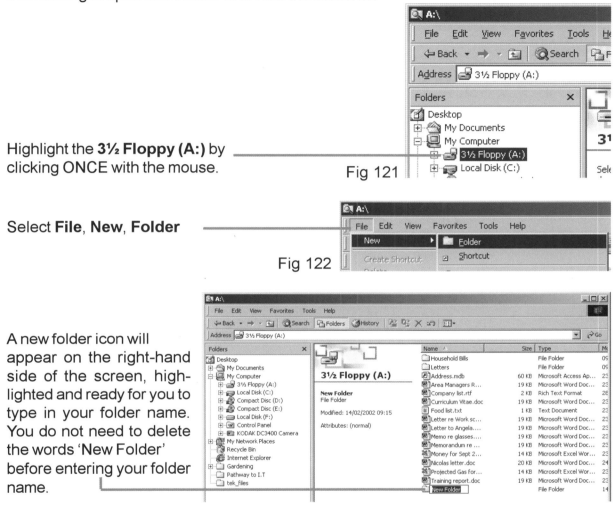

Fig 123

Type in the folder name and press **Enter**.

If the new folder cannot be seen on the left-hand side of the screen, click on the **+** next to the **3½ Floppy (A:)** and the folder with the name you typed in will appear.

You have now created a folder that you can move or copy files into.

TASK

1.   Create a new folder on the 3½ Floppy (A:) called **Wedding plans**.

Creating Sub-folders (Sub-directories)

A sub-folder is a folder within another folder.

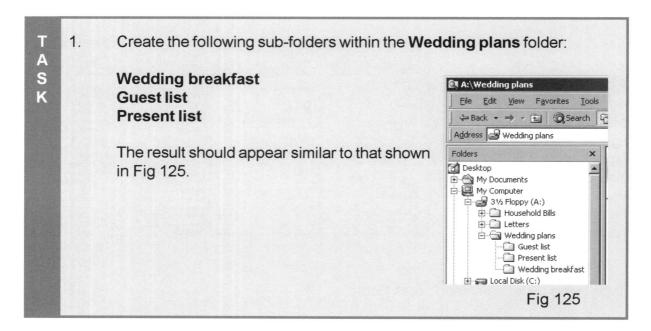

The **Address bar** displays what has been selected.
In this example: **A:\Wedding plans**
the **Wedding plans** folder on the floppy disk drive (A:)
has been selected.

Highlight the folder in which you want to create the new folder.

Fig 124

Select **File**, **New**, **Folder**.

The new folder icon will appear on the right-hand side of the screen, highlighted and ready for you to type in your folder name.

Type in the folder name and press **Enter**.

On the left-hand side of the screen, click on the **+** next to the folder. This will show the new sub-folder you have created.

T A S K

1. Create the following sub-folders within the **Wedding plans** folder:

   Wedding breakfast
   Guest list
   Present list

   The result should appear similar to that shown in Fig 125.

Fig 125

When displaying a list of files in **Windows Explorer** the complete file name may not be visible. This is indicated by a series of dots at the end of the visible file name. To dispay the name in full move the mouse pointer between the headings **Name** and **Size** where a small black line is displayed.

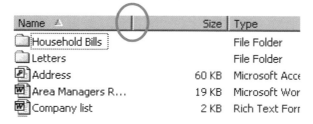

The mouse will change to a double-headed arrow. Double-click and all the file names will be displayed in full.

Moving Files And Folders

You may wish to move files or folders from one location to another.

Select the file or folder you wish to move (cut).

> Click **Edit**
> Click **Cut**

Fig 126

or

Click on the **Cut** button on the **Toolbar**.

Click on the folder or drive to where you wish to move the file or folder (left pane). Check the **Address Bar** to ensure that the correct location has been selected.

> Click **Edit**
> Click **Paste**

Fig 127

or

Click on the **Paste** button on the **Toolbar**.

This will move a file or folder from its original location to its new location.

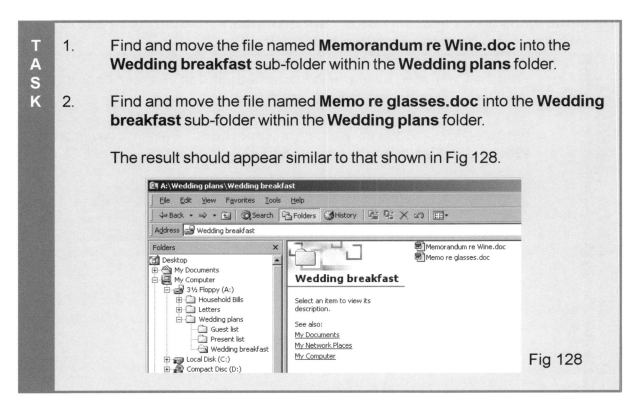

TASK

1. Find and move the file named **Memorandum re Wine.doc** into the **Wedding breakfast** sub-folder within the **Wedding plans** folder.

2. Find and move the file named **Memo re glasses.doc** into the **Wedding breakfast** sub-folder within the **Wedding plans** folder.

    The result should appear similar to that shown in Fig 128.

Fig 128

Copying Files And Folders

You may wish to copy a file or folder and place the copy into another location. Copying enables duplicate copies of files and folders to be made.

Select the file or folder you wish to copy.

Click **Edit**
Click **Copy**

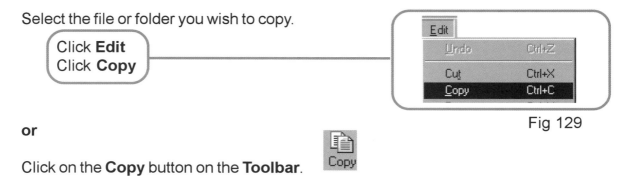

Fig 129

or

Click on the **Copy** button on the **Toolbar**.

Click on the folder or the drive where you wish to place the duplicate file or folder (left pane). Check the **Address Bar** to ensure that the correct location has been selected.

Click **Edit**
Click **Paste**

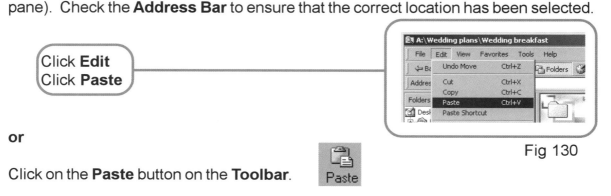

Fig 130

or

Click on the **Paste** button on the **Toolbar**.

This will make a copy of the file or folder in the selected location.

NB   If the icons aren't available select View, Toolbars, Customize to add or remove icons from the Standard buttons toolbar.

TASK

1. Find the file named **Letter re Work schedule.doc**. Place a copy into the **Work** sub-folder within the **Letters** folder.

2. Find the file named **Area Managers Report.doc**. Place a copy into the **Work** sub-folder within the **Letters** folder.

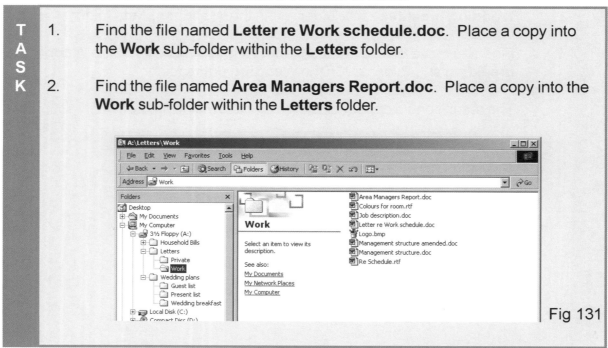

Fig 131

Multiple File Selection

Multiple file selection increases efficiency, allowing the user to move or copy more than one file at a time.

Selecting A Group Of Files Together

Select the first file in the group.

Fig 132

Press and hold the **Shift** key (above the **Ctrl** key) in the lower left-hand corner of the keyboard.

Select the last file in the group
(all the file names in the group will be highlighted).

Fig 133

Release the **Shift** key.

Commands made will apply to all the highlighted files.

**NB   Highlighting mistakes can be de-selected by clicking anywhere in a blank
      area.**

Selecting Multiple Files That Are Not Grouped Together

Click on one of the files that
you wish to select.

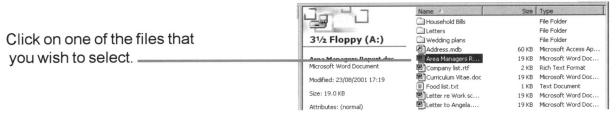

Fig 134

Press and hold the **Control** (**Ctrl**) key on the keyboard.

Click on each of the files you wish to
select, one at a time.

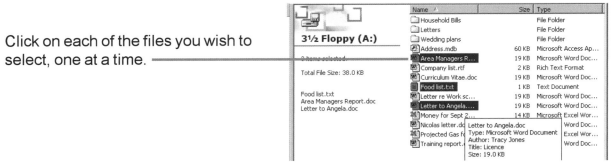

Fig 135

Then release the **Control** (**Ctrl**) key.

Any commands that are now made, ie **copy** or **cut**, will apply to the highlighted files.

NB **Highlighting mistakes can be de-selected one at a time. Press the Ctrl key, click on a highlighted file to de-select it. To de-select all highlighted files, click on a blank area of the screen without presing the Ctrl key.**

| T A S K | 1. | Practise selecting and de-selecting multiple files that are grouped. |
| | 2. | Practise selecting and de-selecting files that are not grouped. |

Renaming Files And Folders

Files and folders can be renamed to reflect their content more accurately or to correct any previous errors in naming.

Renaming Files

Highlight the file you wish to rename.

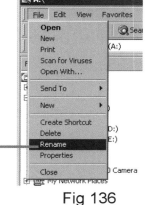

Click **File**, **Rename**.

Fig 136

The file name will be highlighted.
Place the cursor over the selected file name. Place the **I-beam** before the file extension.

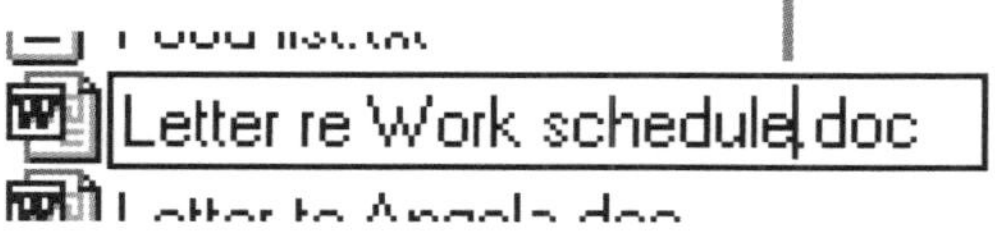

```
Letter re Work schedule.doc
```

Fig 137

Backspace to delete the file name and type in the new name. **You must ensure that the full file extension (including full stop) is left in place.**

Press the **Enter** key to accept the change.

> **TASK**
>
> 1. Change the file name of the document named **Letter re Work schedule.doc** to **Work Schedule 20-09-01.doc**.

Renaming Folders

Highlight the folder you wish to rename.

Click **File**, **Rename**.

The folder is highlighted, enabling you to type in the new folder name. Folders do not require an extension.

Press the **Enter** key to accept the change.

> **TASK**
>
> 1. Change the **Letters** folder to **Communication**.

Deleting Files Or Folders

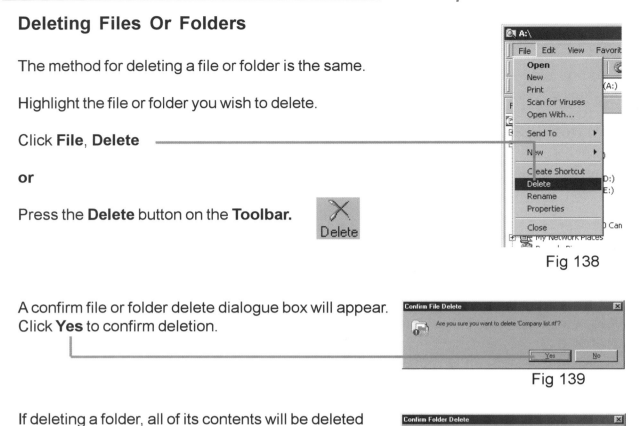

The method for deleting a file or folder is the same.

Highlight the file or folder you wish to delete.

Click **File**, **Delete**

or

Press the **Delete** button on the **Toolbar.**

Fig 138

A confirm file or folder delete dialogue box will appear.
Click **Yes** to confirm deletion.

Fig 139

If deleting a folder, all of its contents will be deleted
including sub-folders and files.

Fig 140

**NB   Files and folders deleted from a floppy disk are not retrievable, but
files and folders deleted from the hard drive (C:) are placed in a folder
called the Recycle Bin, from which they can be retrieved.**

T A S K	1.	Delete the file **Company list.rtf**.
	2.	Delete the folder called **TV Licence** and all its contents.
	3.	Close **Windows Explorer**.

C O N S O L I D A T I O N   E X E R C I S E

1. Change the **Communications** folder back to **Letters**.

2. Create a folder with the name **Meeting** on the A: drive.

3. Create a document with the filename **Corporate Agenda.doc**.
   Save the newly created file into the folder called **Meeting**.

4. Create a new folder with the name **Office Administration**.

5. Place the folder **Meeting** in the folder **Office Administration** so that it now becomes a sub-folder.

6. Practise selecting and de-selecting multiple files.

7. Practise selecting files that are not grouped.

8. Rename the file **Corporate Agenda.doc** to **Corporate ID.doc**.

9. Find the file named **Area Managers Report.doc**. Place a copy into the **Meeting** sub-folder within the **Office Administration** folder.

10. View the folder **Office Administration** within **Windows Explorer**.

11. Delete the folder **Office Administration** and all its contents.

12. Close **Windows Explorer**.

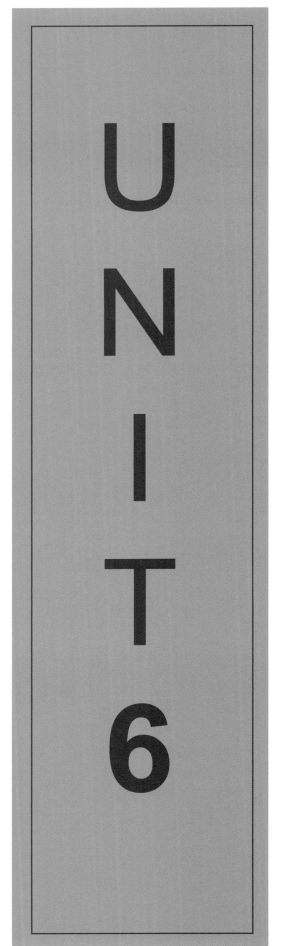

On completion of this unit you will have learnt about and practised using:

File Management Within My Computer
- My Computer Screen
- My Computer Menu Bar

Changing Views
- Changing Style
- Changing File Appearance
- Using My Computer Windows

Creating Folders (Directories) In My Computer
- Creating Folders (Directories)
- Creating Sub-Folders (Sub-directories)
- Moving Files And Folders
- Copying Files And Folders
- Copying Files And Folders By Dragging And Dropping
- Moving Files And Folders By Dragging And Dropping
- Renaming Files And Folders
- Deleting Files And Folders

File Management Within My Computer

Double-click the **My Computer** icon on the **Desktop**

or

Position the mouse over the **My Computer** icon.

Click the right mouse button.

Click **Open** from the menu.

Fig 141

Fig 142

My Computer Screen

My Computer is useful for viewing the contents of a single folder or drive. Their contents are displayed in a new window. **My Computer** gives an immediate view of the different disk storage devices, **Control Panel** and **Printers** (Fig 143). The **My Computer** window may need to be resized so that all the icons are visible.

Title Bar

Menu Bar

Toolbar
(same as Explorer)

Address Bar

Fig 143

My Computer Menu Bar

From the **My Computer Menu Bar** there are a number of familiar (and some not so familiar) options from which to alter the display of the information in your window.

The **Favorites** menu will give you access to the Internet from the saved web pages you have stored.

An interesting, helpful and somewhat humorous feature is the **Tip of the Day** option.

To turn this feature on select: **View**, **Explorer Bar**, **Tip of the Day** (shown in Fig 144).

Displayed in a window at the foot of the screen, this option provides an anecdote on how you can achieve an outcome using a quick-key shortcut or some other useful and efficient method.

Fig 144

As we have seen previously, selecting **Tools**, **Folder Options** will activate the **Folder Options** dialogue box as shown in Fig 145.

Clicking the **View** tab will provide options for changing the view within the folder window. **Advanced settings:** provides yet further options to alter the way information is displayed in the folder window.

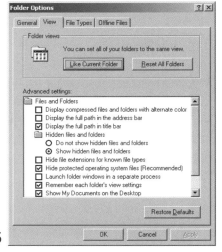

Fig 145

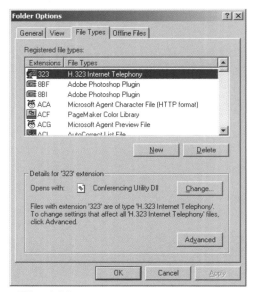

Fig 146

File types contain a list of file extensions and their accompanying names that have been registered to the computer.

Explained briefly in Fig 146 are the file extension details and what software application that particular file extension belongs to.

Click the **New** button to add an extension to the list, or **Advanced** to change the extension icon, to edit or to remove it. **Please do not do this in the centre.**

Offline Files are useful if you are part of a network. Here you can organise your computer to download files from the network, so that they can be used while you are not connected to the network (offline) Fig 147.

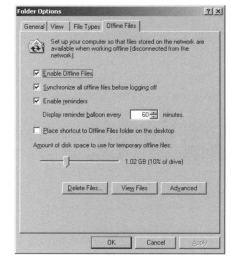

Fig 147

T A S K	1.	Open the **My Computer** window.
	2.	Activate the **Tip of the Day** option.
	3.	Access the **Folder Options** dialogue box. Ensure the **General** tab is selected. From **Web View**, make sure the **Enable Web content in folders** radio button is on. Click **OK**.
	4.	Click the **View** tab from the **Folder Options Dialogue** box. In the **Advanced Settings** window, tick the check box **Display the Full path in title bar**. Click **Apply**, **OK**.

Changing Views

Changing Style

As with **Windows Explorer**, the **My Computer** window can be viewed using **Web View** or **Browse Folder**. Each is achieved in exactly the same way.

Click **Tools**, **Folder Options** then select **Web View**, **Enable Web content in folders** or **Use Windows classic folders**.

Changing File Appearance

As with **Windows Explorer**, the file appearance in the **My Computer** window can be changed in exactly the same way by clicking on the **View** icon.

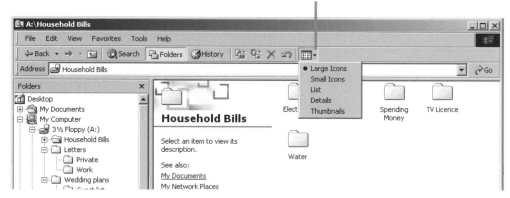

Fig 148

| T A S K | 1. | Practise changing the style and the file appearance. Select **Use Windows** classic folders and **Large Icons** before moving on. |

As previously discussed, you can view **My Computer** using the **Web View** section as with **Windows Explorer**. However, the **Browse Folders** option will enable you to apply settings relating to the way folders and their contents are viewed in **My Computer**.

From the **Tools** menu select, **Folder Options** to display the **Folder Options** dialogue box.

From the **Browse Folder** section, click on the **Open each folder in the same window** radio button shown in Fig 149:

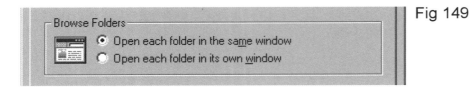

Fig 149

Click **Apply** then **OK**.

Once you return to the **My Computer** window and select a drive, folder or sub-folder, the information accessed will be updated and displayed in a single window.

Use the **Back** or **Forward** buttons on the **Standard toolbar** (Fig 150) to navigate your way through the drives and folders on a computer.

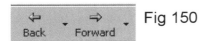

Fig 150

To open each folder in its own window, return to the **Folder Options** dialogue box and click the **Open each folder in its own window** radio button as shown in Fig 151.

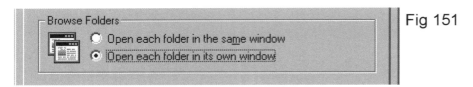

Fig 151

Once again, click **Apply** then **OK**.

Each time a folder is selected and opened on any drive the contents can be viewed in a separate window.

However, if you have many sub-folders within folders you may be viewing many windows!

Using My Computer Windows

As previously described, providing the correct option has been selected, each time a drive or folder is opened in **My Computer**, the content of the selected drive or folder is displayed in the same window.

The **Address bar** displays the name of the selected drive or folder.

Double-click
3½ Floppy (A:)

The content of the floppy disk is shown in the same window. If the last user 'maximised' the window (full screen), click on the **Resize** button.

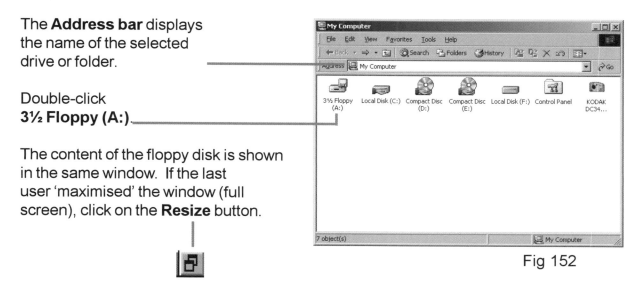

Fig 152

The diagrams in Fig 153 indicate the sequence of windows that will be displayed in the course of accessing the **Gas** sub-folder.

Fig 153

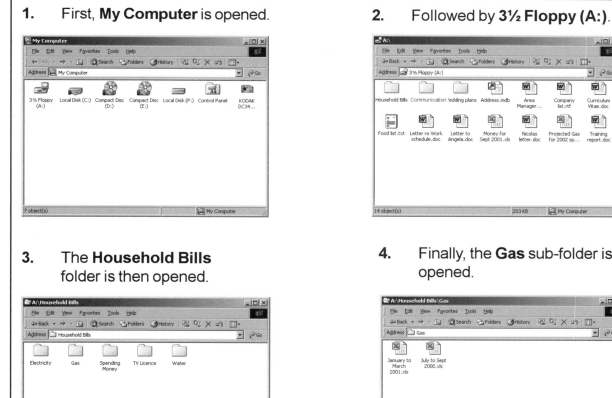

1.   First, **My Computer** is opened.

2.   Followed by **3½ Floppy (A:)**.

3.   The **Household Bills** folder is then opened.

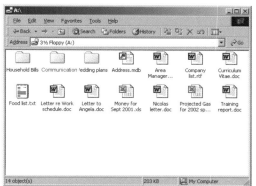

4.   Finally, the **Gas** sub-folder is opened.

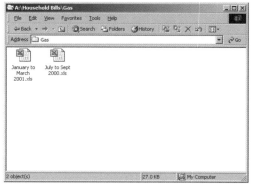

Creating Folders (Directories) In My Computer

Creating Folders (Directories)

Open the **3½ Floppy (A:)**.

Look at the **Address bar** to ensure that the correct folder or drive has been selected.

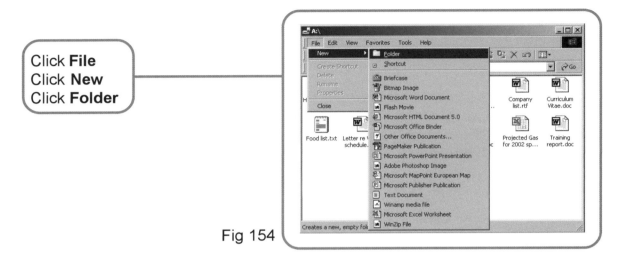

Click **File**
Click **New**
Click **Folder**

Fig 154

A new folder will appear at the bottom of the window, highlighted and ready for you to type in your folder name.

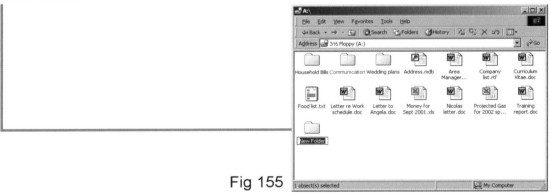

Fig 155

Once you have typed in the folder name, press **Enter**.

T A S K	1.	Create a folder on the 3½ Floppy (A:) called **Gardening**.

Creating Sub-Folders (Sub-directories)

Double-click the folder in which you wish to create the sub-folder.

Look at the **Address bar** to ensure the correct folder or drive has been selected.

Click **File**
Click **New**
Click **Folder**

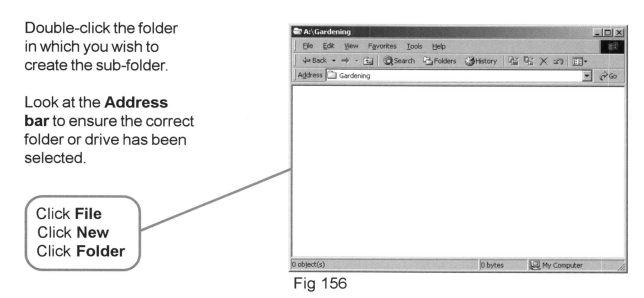

Fig 156

A new folder icon will appear in the window, highlighted and ready for you to overtype the new folder name.

Type in the folder name and **Enter**.

Fig 157

T A S K	1.	Create the following sub-folders within the **Gardening** folder:

Patio
Flowers
Costs

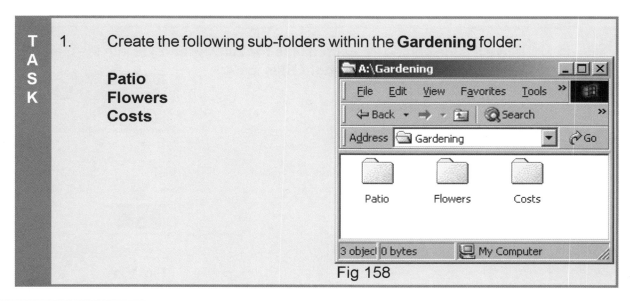

Fig 158

Moving Files And Folders

Select the file or folder you wish to move (cut).

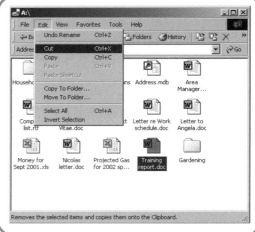

Click **Edit**
Click **Cut**

or

Click on the **Cut** button on the **Toolbar**.

Fig 159

Double-click to open the folder containing the sub-folder you would like to move the file or folder into.

Then double-click to open the sub-folder where you want to move the file or folder to.

Click **Edit**
Click **Paste**

or

Click on the **Paste** button on the **Toolbar**.

NB   If the icons aren't available, select View, Toolbars, Customize to add or remove icons from the Standard toolbar.

Fig 160

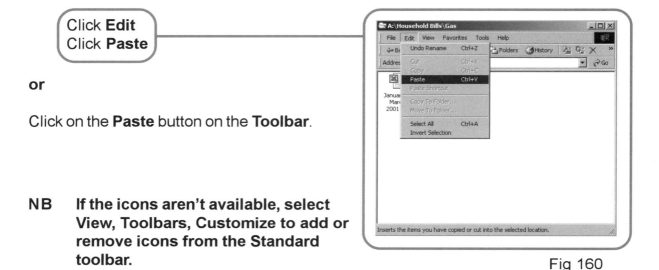

T A S K

1. Move the file named **Projected Gas for 2002 spend.xls** into the **Gas** sub-folder within the **Household Bills** folder.

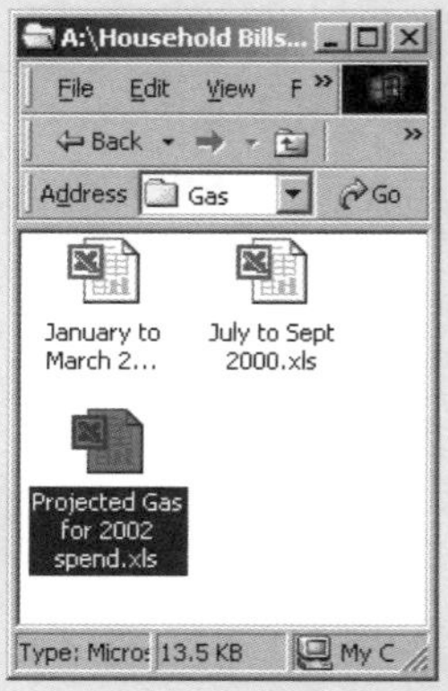

Fig 161

Copying Files And Folders

Select the file or folder that you would like to copy (duplicate).

Click **Edit**
Click **Copy**

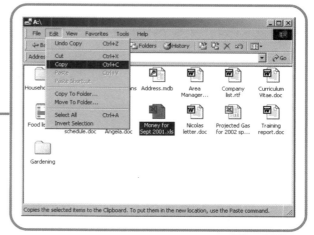

Fig 162

or

Click on the **Copy** button on the **Toolbar**.

Double-click to open the folder containing the sub-folder you would like to copy the file or folder into. Then double-click to open the sub-folder you want to copy the file or folder into.

Click **Edit**
Click **Paste**

or

Click on the **Paste** button on the **Toolbar**.

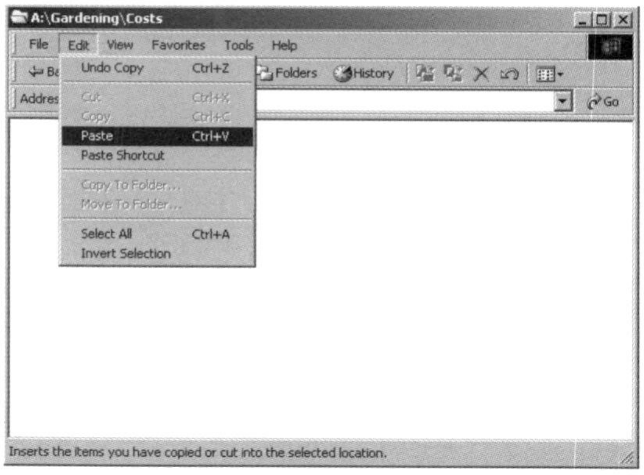

Fig 163

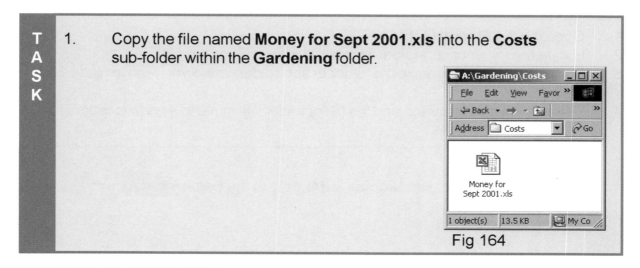

T A S K

1. Copy the file named **Money for Sept 2001.xls** into the **Costs** sub-folder within the **Gardening** folder.

Fig 164

Copying Files And Folders By Dragging And Dropping

Open the **3½ Floppy (A:)**.

Identify the folder or sub-folder where you wish to place the file or folder.

1.   Select the file or folder you want to copy, keeping the left mouse button pressed.
2.   Press the **Ctrl** key (a '+' sign will appear, indicating that the file will be copied instead of being moved).
3.   Drag to the new location.
4.   Release the mouse button - a copy of the file or folder will appear highlighted in its new location.
5.   Release the **Ctrl** key.

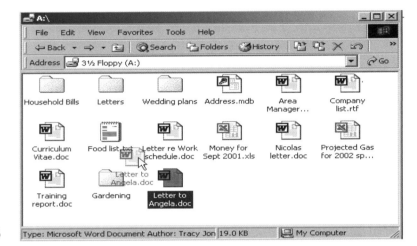

Fig 165

T A S K	1.	Copy the file called **Letter to Angela.doc** to the **Letters** folder on your A: drive.

Moving Files And Folders By Dragging And Dropping

Moving files or folders by dragging and dropping is very similar to copying, but with no need to use the Ctrl key.

1.   Open the **3½ Floppy (A:)**.
2.   Locate the folder or sub-folder where you wish to place the file.
3.   Drag to the new location, ie the folder or sub-folder where you wish to place the file or folder.
4.   Release the mouse button and the file or folder will move to its new location.

T A S K	1.	Move the file called **Nicolas letter.doc** to the **Letters** folder on your A: drive.

Renaming Files And Folders

The methods of renaming files and folders are exactly the same as within **Windows Explorer**.

Deleting Files And Folders

The methods of deleting files and folders are exactly the same as within **Windows Explorer**.

> **T**
> **A**   1.   Close all open windows, including **My Computer**.
> **S**
> **K**

NB It is worth noting tha tif you are moving or copying files across a complicated file structure, it is easier to use Windows Explorer than My Computer as Windows Explorer allows you to expand the folder structures and to clearly see folders, subfolders and files in a much simpler manner.

On completion of this unit you will have learnt about and practised using:

Desktop Icons
- Creating A Desktop Shortcut
- Moving A Shortcut
- Deleting Shortcut Icons
- Backing Up A File Onto A Floppy Disk
- Creating A Back up File On The Same Floppy Disk
- Creating A Back up File From The Hard Disk Onto A Floppy Disk
- Creating A Disk To Disk Copy
- Formatting A Floppy Disk

Finding Files
- Finding A File
- Finding The File By Name
- Finding The File By Date
- Finding The File By The File Type
- Using The Recycle Bin

Desktop Icons

Creating A Desktop Shortcut

Shortcuts of regularly used items can be placed on the **Desktop**, so that the file or programme can be accessed quickly.

Open **Windows Explorer**.

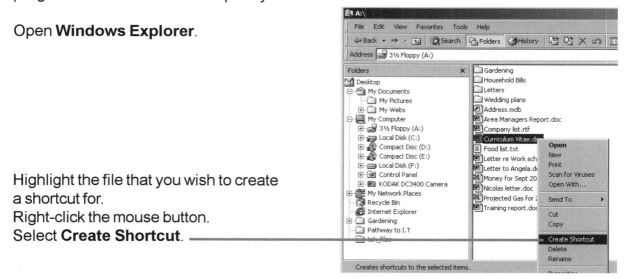

Highlight the file that you wish to create
a shortcut for.
Right-click the mouse button.
Select **Create Shortcut**.

Fig 166

An example of a shortcut is shown below. The small curved arrow at the right of the icon indicates that you are looking at a shortcut. When you create a new shortcut it is named 'Shortcut to..' as a default.

Ensure that your shortcut is highlighted.

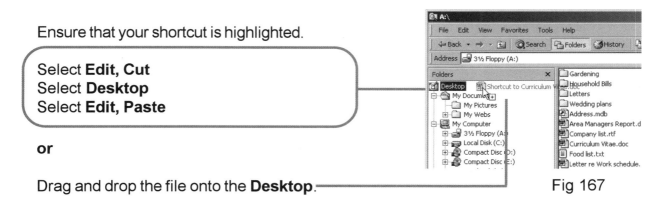

Select **Edit, Cut**
Select **Desktop**
Select **Edit, Paste**

or

Drag and drop the file onto the **Desktop**.

Fig 167

**T
A
S
K**

1.   Create a shortcut file for **Curriculum Vitae.doc**. Place the shortcut on
      the **Desktop**.

Moving A Shortcut

To move the shortcut icons, click and drag
the icons to a different position in the list (Fig 168).

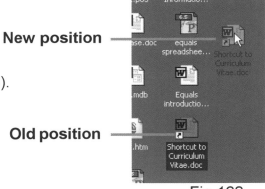

New position

Old position

Fig 168

**NB The icon may not move if Auto Arrange
has been selected. If this is the case,
right-click in a blank area of the
Desktop, select Arrange Icons and
remove the tick against Auto Arrange.**

Deleting Shortcut Icons

Fig 169

When shortcuts are no longer required they can be deleted.

Select the shortcut
Click the right mouse button
Click **Delete**
Click **Yes** to delete the icon

or

Select the shortcut with the left mouse button.

Drag and drop the icon into the **Recycle Bin** icon on the
Desktop.

Fig 170

Deleting a shortcut does not delete the original file. However, if the original file is
renamed, moved or deleted the shortcut will not work.

If a shortcut is created for a file that is stored on a floppy disk, you must ensure that the
floppy disk is inserted into the drive before using the shortcut. If the floppy disk is not
present when the shortcut is double-clicked an error message similar to Fig 171 will appear:

Fig 171

| T A S K | 1. | Practise moving the icons on the **Desktop**. |
| | 2. | Delete the **Curriculum Vitae** shortcut. Do not delete any other shortcuts from the **Desktop**. |

Backing Up A File Onto A Floppy Disk

The internal hard disk is generally a well designed component that can perform reliably for many thousands of hours over several years. However, it is by no means uncommon for individuals and even companies to 'lose' the entire contents of a hard disk due to accidents such as power surges, virus attacks or computer failure. The only way to reduce the risk of a this causing you a big problem is to make duplicate or back up copies of all important files. Ideally, the back up copy should be on a removable disk (floppy, zip or CD) that will allow it to be stored in a safe place. Businesses often have a fire proof safe for this purpose.

Creating A Back Up File On The Same Floppy Disk

Using **Windows Explorer** or **My Computer**, create a folder on the floppy disk called **Backup**.

Select the file. Copy the file you wish to back up and place the copy in the back up folder. Rename the file so that the name indicates it is a back up.

TASK

1. Create a folder called **Back Up** on the 3½ **Floppy (A:)**.

2. Copy the file **Curriculum Vitae.doc** to the **Back Up** folder.

3. Rename the file so that it reads **Curriculum Vitae backup.doc**.

Creating A Back Up File From The Hard Disk Onto A Floppy Disk

Using **Windows Explorer** or **My Computer**, locate the file on the hard drive that you wish to back up to floppy disk.

Select the file. Copy the file you wish to back up. Paste the copy onto the floppy disk.

It is important to remember that floppy disks can only store a limited amount of information compared to the hard disk. If you have a lot of information that you need to back up, it would be worth investigating a larger backup device such as a Zip Drive or other similar device. More information about storage devices is contained later in this Resource Pack.

Creating A Disk To Disk Copy

Insert the disk you wish to copy.
Using **Windows Explorer** or **My Computer**
select **3½ Floppy (A:)**.

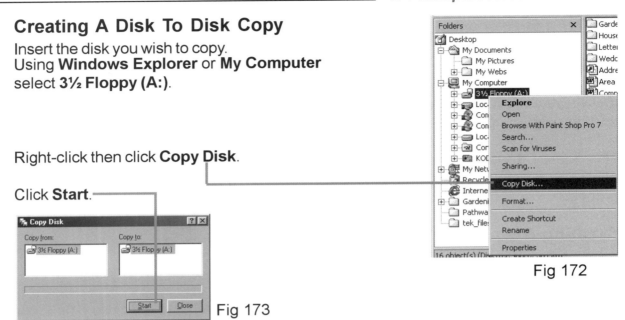

Right-click then click **Copy Disk**.

Click **Start**.

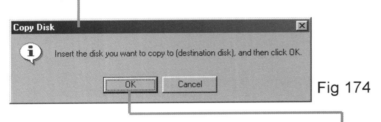

Fig 173

Fig 172

The **Copy Disk** dialogue box will appear once a copy has been made of the floppy disk.

Fig 174

Replace the floppy disk with a blank one. Click **OK**.

Once the disk copying has been completed the dialogue box (Fig 175) will indicate if the copy has been successful.

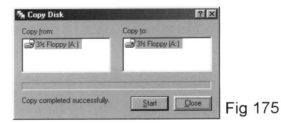

Fig 175

NB   Use a blank disk to copy to - any files on a disk will be overwritten.

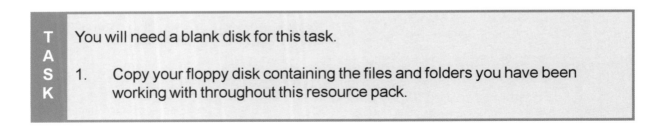

T
A
S
K

You will need a blank disk for this task.

1.   Copy your floppy disk containing the files and folders you have been
        working with throughout this resource pack.

Formating A Floppy Disk

Even though most floppy disks are 'pre-formatted' (prepared for use by the computer), some do need formatting. Formatting is a useful way of clearing all the data from a disk so that you can re-use it. Formatting a disk removes EVERYTHING from your disk.

Using Windows Explorer

Select the **3½ Floppy (A:)**.

Right-click.

Select **Format**.

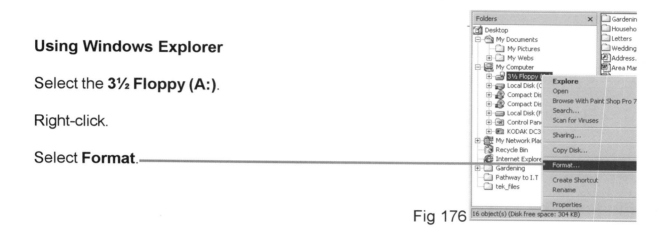

Fig 176

NB   Make sure that 3½ Floppy (A:) is displayed in the Title Bar.

Click **Start**.

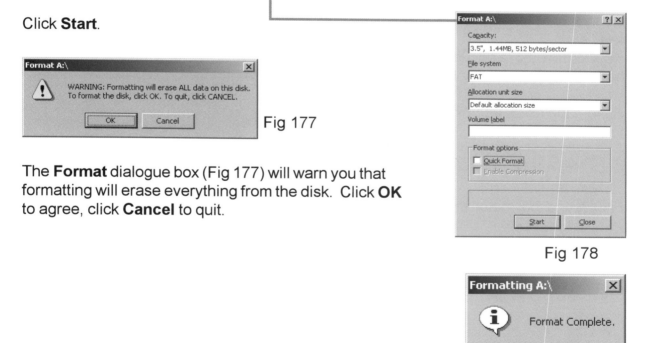

Fig 177

The **Format** dialogue box (Fig 177) will warn you that formatting will erase everything from the disk. Click **OK** to agree, click **Cancel** to quit.

Fig 178

Click **OK**.

Fig 179

T A S K	
	1. Format the copied floppy disk.

Finding Files

Finding A File - Advanced Options

Finding files on a floppy disk or hard drive can take some time if files are not kept in an organised structure. The computer has a search facility to assist.

Click **Start**.

Click **Search**.

Click **For Files or Folders...**.

Finding The File By Name

Click on the **Name & Location** tab.

File names can be typed into the **Search for files or folders named:** text field.
Keywords within a document can be entered in this text field.

Ensure the **Look in:** box shows the **3½ Floppy (A:)**.

Click **Search Now**.

Files found that match the named criteria are displayed here.

The exact location of the file is shown here.

Double-click the file to open it.

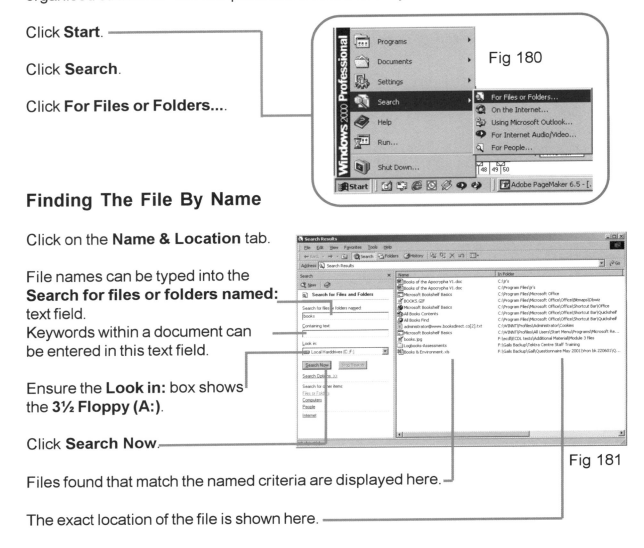

Fig 180

Fig 181

TASK

1. Using the floppy disk you began the ITP module with, find all files that have **July** in the title.

Finding The File By Date

Ensure the **Look in:** box shows the **3½ Floppy (A:)** drive.

Click the **Search Options** link to find files by **Date**, **Type**, **Size** and **Advanced Options**.

Click the **Date** check box.

Select **files Modified**.

Click **between**.

The dates can be changed by clicking the drop-down arrow.

Fig 182

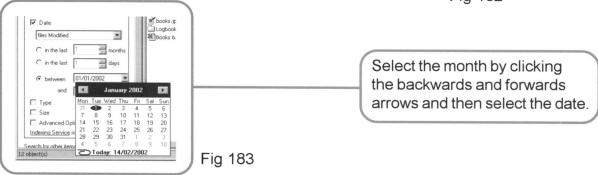

Fig 183

Select the month by clicking the backwards and forwards arrows and then select the date.

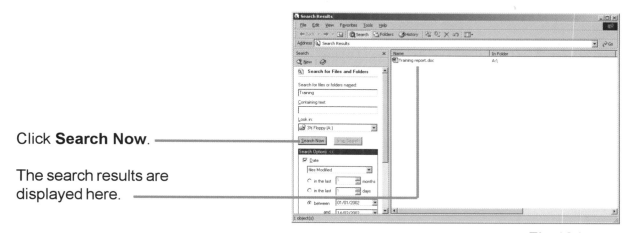

Click **Search Now**.

The search results are displayed here.

Fig 184

T A S K	1.	Find the files that have been modified between 20/02/02 and 22/02/02.

Finding The File By The File Type

Ensure the **Look in:** box shows the **3½ Floppy (A:)** drive.

Click in the **Type** check box.

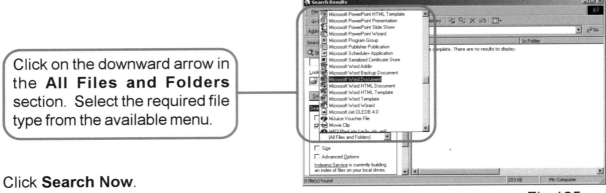

Click on the downward arrow in the **All Files and Folders** section. Select the required file type from the available menu.

Click **Search Now**.

Fig 185

T A S K	1.	Find the files that were created with Microsoft Word and have a .doc file extension.

Being able to locate files using the options available is a useful skill if you have to recover information from a backup - this will ensure you can find the right files that were created at the right time, cutting down on the time you spend checking what is on your backup disks. It also means that you know exactly what to backup in the first place- if you want to back up everything you have done in a single day, the files can be searched for using the date option, making it easier for you to identify and locate the informtion for your backup.

Using The Recycle Bin

Files deleted from a floppy disk are not recoverable, but files deleted from the hard drive are placed into a folder called the **Recycle Bin**. These files will remain in the **Recycle Bin** until you decide to empty it. These files can be restored to their original locations.

Double-click the **Recycle Bin** icon on the **Desktop**.

Fig 186

To Restore A File

Click on the file you wish to restore.
Click **File**.
Click **Restore**.
The file will be restored to its original location.

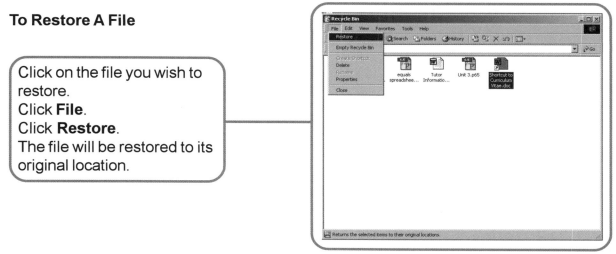

Fig 187

To Empty The Recycle Bin

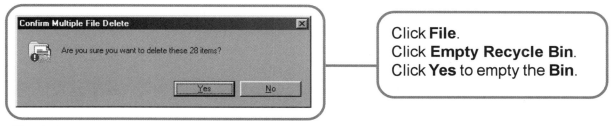

Click **File**.
Click **Empty Recycle Bin**.
Click **Yes** to empty the **Bin**.

Fig 188

NB   The Recycle Bin should be emptied regularly to free up disk space.

TASK

1. Copy the **Curriculum Vitae** file into **My Documents** on the C: drive.

2. Delete the copied file called **Curriculum Vitae** in **My Documents**.

3. Restore the file.

4. Delete the file and empty the **Recycle Bin**.

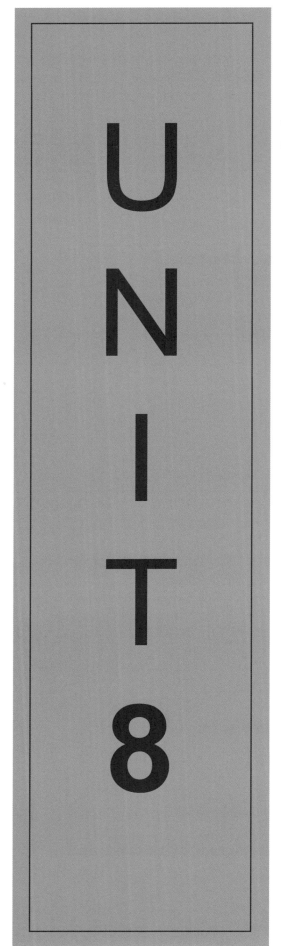

On completion of this unit you will have learnt about and practised using:

Saving Files
- Saving A File Onto A Floppy Disk
- Saving A File To A Folder

Viewing Printer Settings
- Printing From An Installed Printer
- Viewing A Print Job's Progress
- How To Change The Default Printer

Saving Files

Saving A File Onto A Floppy Disk

TASK

1. Open the word processing application.
Click **Start**, **Programs**, **Microsoft Word**.

2. Type in the following text (your line endings may be different):

Word processing is the most widely used computer application and the one which most people are familiar with. It involves the entering and presentation of text.

Text can be moved around and errors corrected easily. Different styles and sizes of text can be used and their layout can be amended without difficulty. Spelling and grammar can be checked by the computer as you go along or after completing documents.

Click **File**.

Click **Save As**.

Click on the **Save in:** drop-down arrow. Select **3½ Floppy (A:)**.

Type the new name into the **File name** box.

Click **Save**.

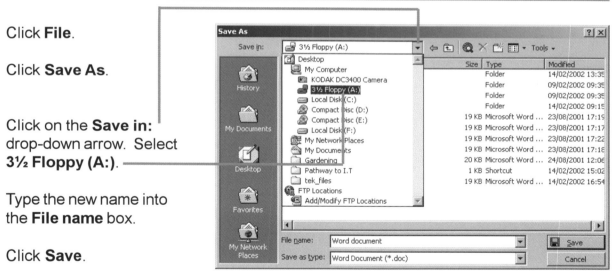

Fig 189

TASK

1. Save the file with the name **Word Document** onto the floppy disk.

Saving A File To A Folder

Click **File**.

Click **Save As**.

Click on the **Save in:**
drop-down arrow, select
3½ Floppy (A:).

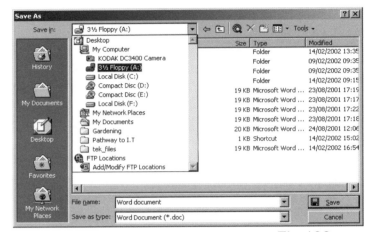

Fig 190

Double-click the folder into which you wish to place the file.

Double-click the sub-folder into which you wish to place the file (if required).

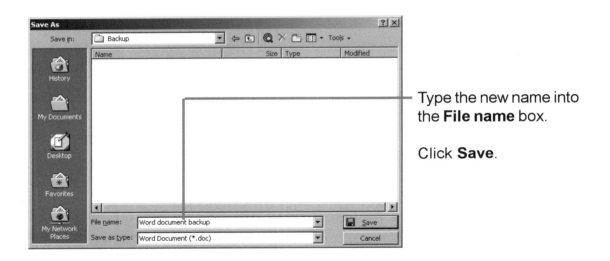

Type the new name into
the **File name** box.

Click **Save**.

Fig 191

T A S K	1.	With the Word document open, save the file as **Word Document Back Up** in the **Backup** folder on the floppy disk.

Viewing Printer Settings

Printing From An Installed Printer

To print a document in the Windows operating environment:

Select the file to be printed.
Click **File**.
Click **Print**.
Click **OK**.

or

Click on the **Print** button on the **Toolbar**.

T A S K	1.	Print the Word document that you have opened on your screen.

Viewing A Print Job's Progress

The computer sends the data to the printer and sometimes this process can take longer than you expect. Many other people may be printing to the same printer, or a large file may be in the process of being printed. Don't add to the frustration by sending multiple copies of the same document.

If the printer receives two or more print jobs at one time, it holds them in the order that they were received. When a print job reaches the top of the line, the spool manager sends the job to the printer.

The spool manager icon will be displayed on the right-hand side of the **Taskbar**.

Fig 192

To activate the spool manager dialogue box as pictured in Fig 193, double-click the **Spool Manager** icon on the **Taskbar**.

Fig 193

From the spool manager, you can view print status information about the print jobs that have been sent to your printer. You can also cancel, pause and resume print jobs by selecting the document and clicking **Document** from the Menu Bar. It is not always possible to cancel a print job if it is only a single page document, depending on the speed of the computer and/or network.

How To Change The Default Printer

Your computer may be on a network that may have more than one choice of printer installed. To change the default printer when working on a document or in an application:

Click **File**.
Click **Print**.

Click on the drop-down arrow next to the **Name:**list box

Select the printer that you wish to send the document to.

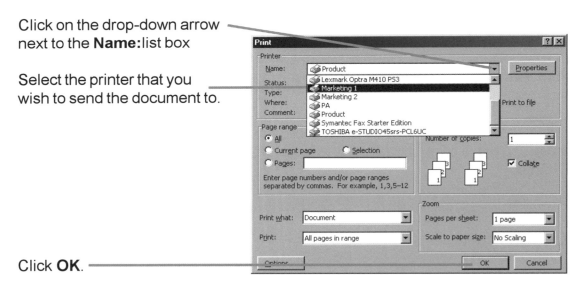

Click **OK**.

Fig 194

T A S K	1.	View the installed printers. Do not change the printer settings.
	2.	Close all applications.

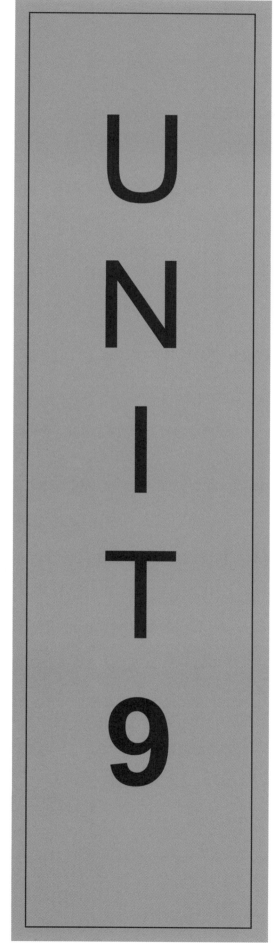

On completion of this unit you will have learnt about:

Data Storage
- Measurements Of Data Storage
- Data Storage Table

Storage Devices
- Floppy Disk
- Zip Disk
- Data Cartridge
- CD-ROM
- CD-R/CD-RW
- DVD

Types of Memory
- RAM
- ROM
- Differences Between RAM And ROM

Saving Data
- The Importance Of Backing Up Data
- What To Back Up
- Save Data To A Hard Disk
- Computer Performance

Data Storage

Measurements Of Data Storage

The following definitions explain the terminology used to identify memory size.

Bit

A shortened term for binary digit. A bit or a binary digit has either the value 1 or 0. It is the smallest unit of data that can be stored within the computer.

Byte

A group of eight bits represents one byte.

Kilobyte (K, KB, KByte)

A unit of storage referring to the memory capacity where 1 KB = 1024 bytes.

Megabyte (M, MB, MByte)

A unit of storage where 1 MB is just in excess of 1 million bytes. Floppy disks have approximately 1.44 MBytes of storage.

Most computer systems have the capacity of their main memory expressed in MBytes.

Gigabytes (G, GB, GBytes)

A unit of storage equal to one thousand MegaBytes. Typically, hard drive storage is expressed in Gigabytes.

Data Storage Table

Storage medium	Surface abrasion	Magnetic fields	Electrostatic discharge	Temperature below 0°C or above 60°C	Humidity below 8% or above 90%	Physical damage
Floppy disk	Data loss if disk surface area exposed	Susceptible to damage even when not actually exposed to atmosphere	Susceptible to damage even when not actually exposed to atmosphere	Disk surface may be affected and drive read/write head may not be able to identify the data	Disk surface may be affected and drive read/write head may not be able to identify the data	May be easily damaged due to thin plastic coating
Hard disk	Disk surface area sealed within a metal case not affected	If metal casing is magnetised, data on disk contained within may be corrupted	Susceptible especially if associated electronic circuits are subjected to discharge	Relatively unaffected	Relatively unaffected	Hard disk damaged if machine moved whilst operational/ switched on
CD-ROM	Much more resilient but could result in data loss where surface is scratched	Not affected by magnetic fields	Not affected by electrostatic discharge	Not affected	Not affected	Extreme damage to the disk surface area will result in data loss
Tape cartridge	Tape normally fully exposed when not in tape drive, easily damaged if exposed to surface abrasion	Easily affected if tape exposed	Susceptible if internal tape is exposed	Operation of tape cartridge may be affected, resulting in tape not moving over tape head	Operation of tape cartridge may be affected, resulting in tape not moving over tape head	Casing much stronger than floppy disk, but could be damaged with extreme force or if tape exposed

Fig 195

Storage Devices

When the computer is shut down, anything stored in volatile memory is lost. On the front of the system unit there is a slot that allows you to use floppy disks and usually a CD drive for compact discs. These types of device are known as removable media or auxilliary storage and there are three types:

- Magnetic disks.
- Magnetic tape.
- Optical storage.

Floppy Disk

Floppy disks are small removable units used in disk drives usually referred to as the A: drive.

Diskettes are 3½" in size and have a hard plastic protective case with a metal cover that slides back when inserted in the disk drive, exposing the magnetic coated disk. Floppy disks are usually high-density double-sided disks with a storage capacity of 1.44 MB. Double density disks have a storage capacity of 720 KB. Floppy disks need to be formatted prior to use, but pre-formatted disks are widely available. Formatting prepares the disk for the type of computer it is to be used in, such as an Apple Macintosh or IBM-compatible PC.

Fig 196

Floppy disks can be protected from being overwritten by a **write-protect notch** that slides across one of the small holes in the disk. Floppy disks require a great deal of care to ensure they are not damaged and to prevent the information held on them from being lost.

Disks should be kept away from all magnetic and heat sources and should be stored carefully in boxes or other dust-free environments. You should not slide back the metal cover and under no circumstances should you touch the magnetic surface.

Floppy disks are a cheap storage medium with a small storage capacity.

Zip Disk

A zip disk looks like a floppy disk. It is a removable magnetic disk capable of storing 100MB or more, of information. A zip drive can be internal or external to the computer. They are very fast and are used to keep back up copies of data files. They are also useful when transferring files from one computer to another. However, these disks are expensive in comparison to floppy disks.

Fig 197

Data Cartridge

This form of data storage is also known as magnetic tape and is slower and cheaper than other magnetic storage devices. It is used mainly for backing up data in large organisations. It is very reliable. The consequence of using magnetic tape means that data has to be read sequentially from start to finish until the required information is located. Files cannot be immediately accessed as they can from disks, which use random access to locate the required data. The drives used in PCs for this storage medium are often referred to as **tape-streamers**.

Fig 198

CD-ROM (Compact Disk Read-Only Memory)

CD-ROMs are optical storage and are round discs resembling an audio CD. Software is usually distributed on CD-ROM and the information is burned onto the surface of the disc. A laser beam in the drive unit reads this information. CD-ROMs have a large capacity, typically 650 MB (which is more than 500 floppy disks). They are cheap and extremely reliable.

Fig 199

CD-R/CD-RW

A CD-writer (for CD-R discs) or rewriter drive (for CD-RW discs) is required for these types of CDs. Like standard CD-ROMs, a CD-R or a CD-RW can store up to 650 MB of data, which makes it an ideal format for making backups of your valuable data.
CD-R (Compact Disc Recordable) and CD-RW (Compact Disc Rewritable) are new forms of compact disc, where you can save your own data onto the disc. CD-R is known as a WORM format (Write Once, Read Many). You can only write information to the disc once and it cannot be deleted or overwritten as with floppy disks.

Fig 200

You can write information to CD-RWs many times until maximum storage capacity has been reached. You can then format it to delete data, enabling new data to be stored.

DVD

DVD (Digital Digital Versatile Disc) is an optical storage disk similar to a CD but with a capacity of over 4.7 GB. A DVD can hold a full-length film with high quality video and audio. DVD drives read existing CD-ROMs and music CDs and are compatible with installed sound and video cards. DVDs can be used for backing up data if a special DVD writer and compatible disks are used. This is has not been a very widely used backup method due to the cost of the DVD writer and the disks.

Fig 201

Types of Memory

Computers use memory in different ways. They use storage memory to save files and folders that you create, and to store their programs and applications. This is the type of memory you will be most familliar with after working through this Resource Pack.

However, computers use a different type of memory (working memory) to process instructions and to carry out the instructions you give them. It is easy to confuse storage memory and working memory as neither are things that you can see or touch.

Types of Working Memory

Computers have two main types of working memory. These are called **RAM** (Random Access Memory) and **ROM** (Read Only Memory).

RAM

RAM is used when operating the computer - program instructions and information are temporarily stored in the computer RAM until you decide that you want to save the information permanently (when it would then be saved and stored in the storage memory - to the Hard Disk or Floppy Disk).

The computer RAM is called so because the computer can access the information it is temporarily storing in any order - rather like a CD player which can skip through the CDs and play them in the order you want the hear them.

RAM is *volatile* memory – when power is switched off, the information held in RAM is lost.

Hard drives and floppy disks are also random access devices, but they aren't 'working' memory like RAM they are simply storage devices that act like digital filing cabinets.

ROM

Read Only Memory (ROM) are small memory chips in the computer which contain information that the computer can read (Read Only). This type of memory is used to hold instuctions and programmes to help the computer to do something - one example is the POST (Power On Self Test) which checks the main computer components in turn as the power is switched on to ensure that each one is working. If one of the checked components is not working - the POST chip returns an error message (usually a series of beeps).

ROM is *non-volatile* memory and therefore does not lose any information when the power is switched off.

Saving Data

The Importance Of Backing Up Data

Backing up your files is the most effective way to avoid losing data. Having recent copies of your work ensures that you will be able to restore or get back important documents quickly if problems should occur with your computer or disk drive.

Backing up important information is similar to taking a photocopy of important documents - if the information changes it is a good idea to get another copy - or take another backup. This is more important for business users as the information they have on their computers could be crucial - but if you do have important documents or things of sentimental value on your computer as a home user a backup is also a good insurance policy.

What To Back Up

There are two main strategies for backing up your data. The first strategy is to **back up everything on each hard drive**. This provides a very high level of security. For smaller offices and machines with smaller hard drives, this isn't too dramatic. However, hard disk sizes (and file sizes) can be vast and for larger offices or organisations with lots of data, backing up everything can be an expensive and time-consuming proposition.

Backing up your entire hard disk means that if you ever have a disk or machine failure, you can restore the entire contents of the drive in one easy process.

Most of the data on your hard disk consists of operating system files and major applications. These files are usually restorable from the original software CD ROM and generally it's not absolutely necessary to back them up, so a second strategy for typical users is to **back up your e-mail files, word processor files, databases, web bookmarks and any other files you directly create** to provide you with sufficient back ups to make recovery possible in the event of a problem.

Save Data To A Hard Disk

As well as saving work to the A: Drive or floppy disk, home users can save their work to the C: Drive or hard disk (this is for information only; please save your work to floppy disk).

Computer Performance

A computer's performance is determined by several factors.

The first is the type of processor and its speed. There are several different processors available such as Intel's Pentium and Celeron and AMD's Athlon and Duron processors. These all have varying clock speeds measured in megahertz; the higher the clock speed, the faster the processor.

The second factor to affect the performance of the computer is the amount of RAM available. The more RAM available, the less the computer has to access the slower storage devices such as the hard disk or CD-ROM. RAM can be upgraded from 32 MB to 64 MB, 128 MB, 256 MB etc to give increased performance.

The third factor is the size and speed of the hard disk. The larger the hard disk, the more you will be able to store on it. Although modern hard disks have very large storage capacities it is still important to keep an eye on how much free hard disk space there is, as the more free space you have, the faster your computer will be able to work. Hard disk access time is also important in determining the performance of a computer. The quicker the access time, the faster the data retrieval.

T A S K

Answer the following questions in your own words:

1. What does the acronym RAM stand for?

2. What is the common size of a floppy disk?

3. What is the storage capacity of a floppy disk?

Check your answers on page 172.

C O N S O L I D A T I O N   E X E R C I S E

On a separate sheet of paper, attempt the answer the following:

1. How many bits are there in a byte?

2. Approximately how many megabytes of storage space are contained on a floppy disk?

3. What is the average size (in inches) of a floppy disk?

4. Other than a floppy disk, name two other types of storage device that can be used to save your work.

5. What do the acronyms RAM and ROM mean? In simple terms, state the difference between the two.

6. Why is it considered so important to back up your work on a regular basis?

7. Name two factors that influence the performance of your computer.

8. Auxiliary storage devices are broken down into three main categories; can you name two?

Check your answers on page 172.

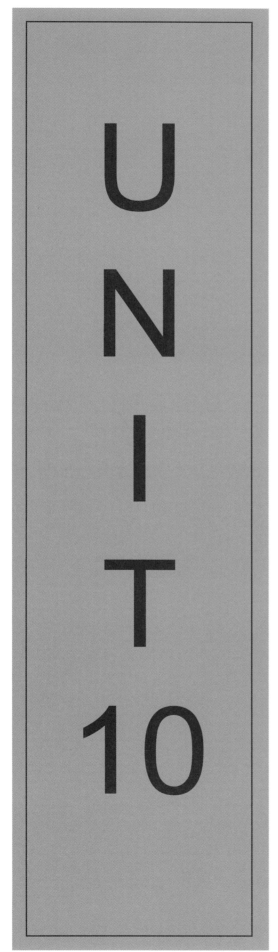

On completion of this unit you will have learnt about:

Software
- Types Of Software
- Operating Systems Software
- Application Software
- Multimedia
- Set Software to Automatically Save

Software

Types Of Software

There are two categories of software: systems software and applications software. Systems software is the main driving program of the computer, without an operating system your PC would be virtually useless; applications software are the specialist programs that enable the computer to perform in a given way, eg like a word processor (Microsoft Word) or enabling you to fly a space ship and shoot at asteroids (Games Software).

Operating Systems Software

This includes the operating system used by the PC, such as MS-DOS, Windows 98, Windows 2000, Unix and Linux. The operating system (OS) is the software that controls the hardware and runs the applications.

When the PC is switched on, the operating system runs through a configuration process to check that all required components are installed such as the hard disk and floppy disk. This is known as the 'boot up' process.

Some operating systems, like Windows, are known as GUI (Graphical User Interface, pronounced 'gooie') as they use menus and small pictures (icons) to make the software more user-friendly. Fig 202 shows an example of a Windows 95 GUI environment.

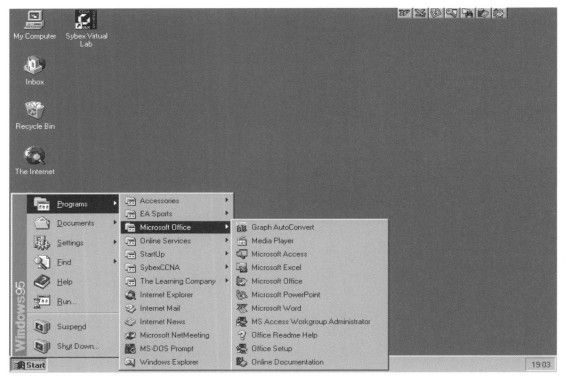

Fig 202

To use the operating system on your computer (assuming you are using Microsoft software), use the mouse to point to the **Start** button in the bottom left corner of the screen.

Click once with the left mouse button and a menu will appear.

Any menu items which include a further sub-menu will appear with a small black arrow pointing to the right.

By pointing the mouse at an item with a sub-menu, the sub-menu will appear.

The small images with text are called 'icons'. When located on the **Desktop**, these icons provide shortcuts to open software applications.

To access the software application, use two successive clicks on the left mouse button (double-click), ensuring that the mouse pointer is hovering over the required icon.

To identify which version of operating software you are using, notice the name appears here:

The version in this example is Microsoft Windows 2000.

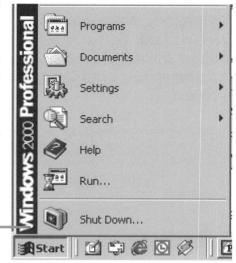

Fig 203

Application Software

This is the term given to the programs that enable the computer to perform in a given way.

Word Processing

Word processing (WP) is the application software used to enter and manipulate text. This text can be formatted in many different ways, including underlining, emboldening, italicising, enlarging or reducing font size (character size), and then saved and printed. Pictures and images can be incorporated and professional looking documents are easily produced. Spelling and grammar can be checked by most word processing software. Text can be easily inserted, deleted and moved. Microsoft Word and Lotus WordPro are examples of Word processing software.

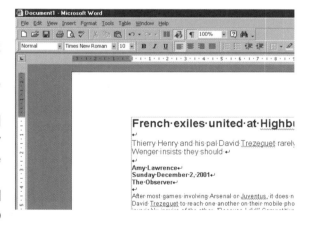

Fig 204

Fig 204 represents an example of a word processed document using Microsoft Word.

Spreadsheet

Spreadsheet (SS) is the application software used primarily for numbers and graphs. It consists of a large grid into which you enter data and text and use formulae to perform calculations. When changes are made to the raw data, the calculated fields are automatically recalculated. Spreadsheets are fast and accurate and are often used in accounting for budget sheets, forecasting, payroll and balance sheets. Graphs such as pie charts and bar charts can be produced. Microsoft Excel and Lotus 123 are examples of spreadsheet software.

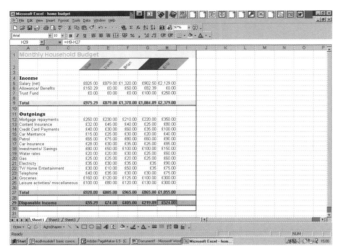

Fig 205 shows an example of a spreadsheet from Microsoft Excel.

Fig 205

Specialist payroll and accounting packages are also available, such as Sage Payroll and Pegasus Accounts.

Database

Database (DB) is the application software that allows the storage of records in an organised manner, such as a catalogue. It is an electronic filing system that can be searched, retrieved, changed and sorted quickly and accurately. Databases are organised records consisting of data that has been 'input' into fields. For example, an address database has one record for each person; each record has a field for name, a separate field for street and another field for postcode etc. Microsoft Access and Lotus Approach are examples of database software.

Fig 206 shows an example of a table of records in a Microsoft Access database.

Address : Table

Name	Street	Town	County	Postal Area
Elaina Briton	23 grange Road	Sheldon	Birmingham	B26 7HG
Janet Riley	8 Woodville Close	Lower Earley	Berkshire	RG6 7EE
Sarah Green	1 Fairley Avenue	Camberley	Surrey	GU17 2DP
Brian Whitaker	99 Ash Close	Chatham	Kent	CT9 2TS
Joseph Leader	45 Jordan Lane	Earley	Berkshire	RG5 1SL

Fig 206

Presentation Graphics

Presentation graphics is the application software that allows you to create, organise and design effective presentations, either by printing onto overhead transparencies, producing 35 mm slides or by running the software as an automated slide show on the PC screen or through a projector. Microsoft PowerPoint and Lotus Freelance are examples of presentation graphics software.

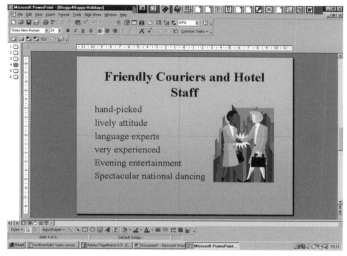

Fig 207 shows an example of a slide from a Microsoft PowerPoint presentation.

Fig 207

Desktop Publishing

Desktop publishing (DTP) is the application software that allows you to create professional looking manuals and brochures. Whilst word processors can perform most of the DTP functions, large publishing houses use dedicated DTP packages. Microsoft Publisher and Adobe PageMaker are examples of desktop publishing software.

Fig 208 shows an example of a Microsoft Publisher document.

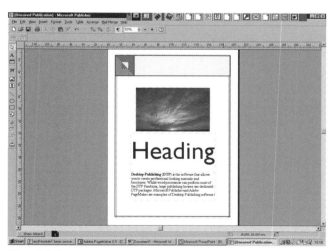

Fig 208

Graphic/Image Manipulation

Drawing and graphic/image manipulation software packages vary from simple-to-use programs, such as Microsoft Paint and Paint Shop Pro, to more sophisticated pieces of software such as Adobe Illustrator and PhotoShop.

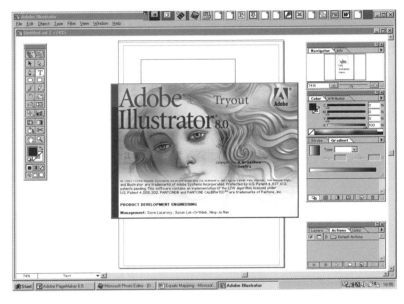

Fig 209

Sophisticated Computer Aided Design (CAD) packages such as AutoCAD 2000 can be used to produce detailed engineering drawings.

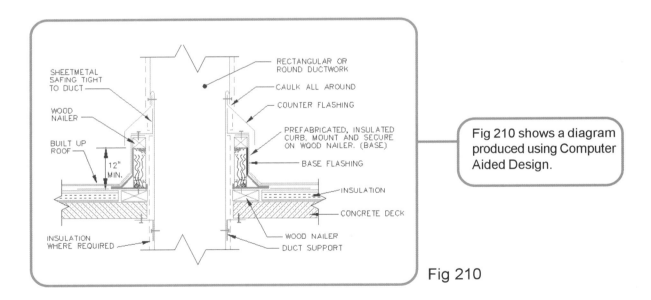

Fig 210 shows a diagram produced using Computer Aided Design.

Fig 210

To view any of the software applications available on your computer, click on the **Start** button then go to **Programs** to view the sub-menu.

Multimedia

Multimedia software is also available combining sound, text, video and images with user interaction, such as games software and music generation software. Web design/authoring software is available to produce web pages and web sites. Common Web authoring applications include Microsoft FrontPage and Macromedia Dreamweaver.

Multimedia is built on the simple principle of using a mixture of different media. However, it now extends beyond the original concept into the world of animation, 3-dimensional images and virtual reality software.

The word 'multimedia' is derived from the mixing together of two words: MULTIple and MEDIA .

Microsoft PowerPoint also contains elements of multimedia.

Set Software To Automatically Save

Access the Microsoft Word application and from the main menu **Select Tools**, **Options**.

From the **Options** dialogue box click the **Save** tab.

Ensure the **Save AutoRecover Info every:** check box is ticked, then using the arrows, or typing directly into the text field, state the time in which your work will be saved periodically.

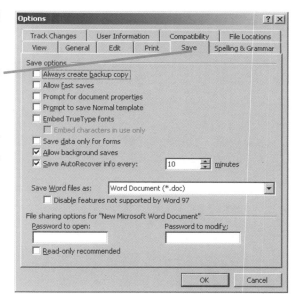

Fig 211

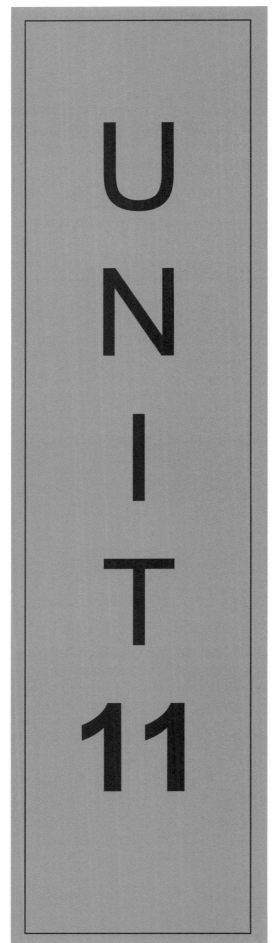

On completion of this unit you will have learnt about:

Networks
- LAN And WAN
- The Telephone Network In Computing
- Facsimile Machine
- Video Conferencing
- Electronic Mail

E-mail And The Internet
- Creating E-mail Messages In Outlook Express
- Sending E-mail Messages
- The Internet
- The World Wide Web

Computers
- Computers In The Home
- Computers At Work Or In Education
- Computers In Daily Life

Society and Computers
- E-commerce

Health And Safety
- Creating A Good Working Environment
- Cleaning Computer Components
- Computers And Legal Requirements
- Management Of Health And Safety At Work Regulations
- Hazardous Substances
- Health And Safety At Work Act 1974

Security
- Security
- Ways In Which Viruses Are Distributed
- Anti-virus Software
- Fire Precautions
- Copyright
- Data Protection Act

Networks

LAN And WAN

There are two types of information network: Local Area Network (LAN) and Wide Area Network (WAN).

Some of the advantages of networking computers together include:

*   Shared resources - one printer can be shared amongst many computers.
*   Shared files - data can be regularly updated in one central place.
*   User groups can be created (usually groups of people with similar job roles and access levels can be set for increased security.
*   Information/data kept electronically is more secure.
*   Information/data can be backed up (copied) in one central place regularly.
*   Files can be accessed from another location.
*   Better control over sensitive information.

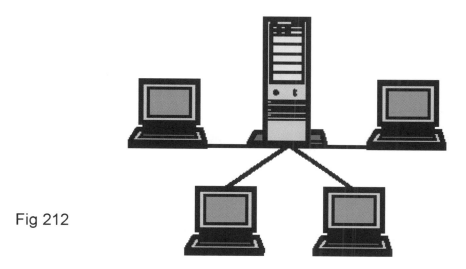

Fig 212

A LAN is a network which connects computers and peripherals within a room, building or other locally confined area. LANs usually have cables that connect the computers together. A local area network without cables that uses high frequency radio waves or infrared beams is known as a Local Area Wireless Network (LAWN).

Each user has their own PC and upon switching on the computer will be faced with a 'log- on' screen requesting security information such as a username and password. On entering this information into the computer, the system will either accept or decline the information. A full list of users and passwords will be held on the system to eliminate unauthorised access to information held. There are increasingly innovative ways to identify users trying to log onto a network or computer systems - even now checking parts of the body such as the eye (as each person's iris is unique - this is known as **biometric security**).

The network may have a 'server', which is a high specification computer used to store all information/data created and saved by users. Users will only be able to access this information if their log-on credentials were accepted.

A WAN connects computers over a wide area, spanning several towns or even countries. This network uses telephone lines, satellite dishes or radio waves to transmit data and information. A WAN is beneficial where users are in multiple locations and so cannot be linked by cables. The Internet is a very large WAN.

The Telephone Network In Computing

Network Technologies

These technologies allow people and computers to communicate with one another by using standardised connection procedures known as protocols.

When a computer sends information to another computer via a telephone line, it needs to be able to convert the digital computer signals to analogue telephone signals. Digital signals have two distinct states whilst analogue signals, such as sound waves, continuously vary.

The equipment used to convert the signals from digital to analogue and vice versa is a **modem**, which is the abbreviation for **mo**dulator/**dem**odulator. The speed at which a modem works is known as the baud rate and this is measured in bits per second (bps) or Kilobits per second (Kbps). The current maximum baud rate that can be transmitted over the public telephone network is 56 Kbps or 56 k baud.

Fig 213

An external modem

Fig 214

An internal modem

An ISDN (Integrated Services Digital Network) line allows data to be transmitted over the line without the need for conversion. The transfer speed of a single line is 64 Kbps; a dual line has a speed of 128 Kbps.

Broadband

The term 'broadband' refers to any type of transmission technique that carries several data channels over a common wire. DSL (Digital Subscriber Line) services, for example, combine separate voice and data channels over a single telephone line - voice fills the low end of the frequency spectrum and data fills the high end. Broadband connections allow high speed data transfer and so enable home users to stream live video or download large files.

ATM

Asynchronous Transfer Mode is a high-speed networking standard designed to support both voice and data communications. ATM operates at the data link layer over either fibre or twisted-pair cable.

DSL

Digital Subscriber Line (DSL) services typically offered today range in performance from 128 Kbps to 1.544 Mbps. It can be difficult to pin down precise speed numbers for DSL because of the many variations in equipment.

DSL is also a distance-sensitive technology and that complicates the performance picture even further. The bandwidth available to a home user, for example, depends significantly on the length of cabling running from the home to the provider's facilities as well as the electrical quality of that line.

CONSOLIDATION EXERCISE

On a separate sheet of paper, write the full descriptions of the following acronyms.

1. ATM

2. DSL

3. LAN

4. WAN

5. ISDN

6. What does the abbreviation 'modem' stand for?

7. Provide a brief description of what the term 'broadband' means.

Check your answers on page 173.

Facsimile Machine

A facsimile (fax) machine (Fig 215) is a device that sends and receives printed pages over the telephone line by converting them into electrical signals using an optical scanner which digitises the page. Fax modems send and receive fax transmissions to and from fax machines or other fax modems, rather than to or from a computer. These transmissions must be stored on disk files. Fax modems can be internal or external to the computer.

Facsimile machine

Fig 215

Telex machines were the first real-time data communications terminals used for sending and receiving messages. Each user is given a telex code and a teleprinter, which consists of a keyboard and printer. There is no monitor, so all messages are printed onto hard copy. Transmission rate is slow, at approximately six characters per second.

Video Conferencing

Video conferencing provides the opportunity to have face-to-face communication remotely, using the Internet. The participants of the conference or meeting need to have access to a computer with software, video camera or web cam and a microphone to capture sound.

The meeting/conference needs to be pre-arranged. It provides all the elements of a meeting inlcuding being able to view body language and other non-verbal communication. However, it saves travelling time for the participants. It is now widely used for meetings, and as a teaching/learning tool in classrooms.

Electronic Mail

Electronic mail (e-mail) allows one person to send a message to any number of other people via the computer, quickly and conveniently. E-mail systems can be internal on a network or worldwide via the Internet and, unlike a telephone call, you are not dependent on the other person being available at the time of sending. You have the advantage of being able to send and receive e-mail messages at cheaper times of the day, calls being charged at local rate, with some service providers offering free phone calls.

An e-mail can be easily sent to several recipients or forwarded to other recipients and when replying to an e-mail you can attach your reply to the original message. You can forward e-mails to different people and you can attach documents such as word processing files or graphics files to e-mails.

Requirements for an e-mail system are: an electronic communication link with the other computers on a network, such as a telephone system described above, a modem, communications software and an Internet Service Provider who will allocate you an e-mail address. Microsoft Outlook and Netscape Composer are examples of communications software.

Fig 216 is an example of the Microsoft Outlook e-mail management software.

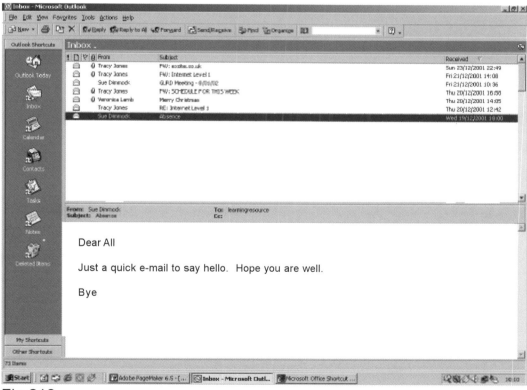

Fig 216

On the left there is a menu of shortcuts from which you can select your chosen option. The option being displayed in Fig 216 is the **Inbox**.

E-mail And The Internet

Creating E-mail Messages In Outlook Express

To create a new mail message, use either of the methods below:

Click on **File**, **New**, **Mail message** from the **Menu Bar**, **or**

Click on the **New Mail** button on the **Toolbar**.

Fig 217

This will activate a new message window for your message:

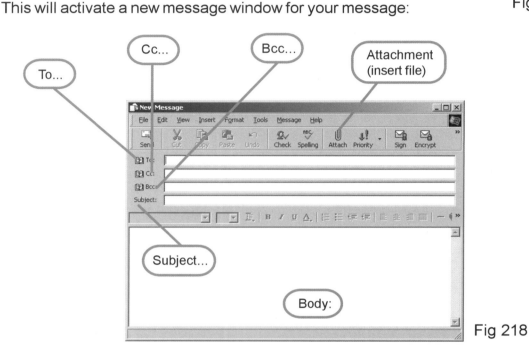

Fig 218

Sending E-mail Messages

When sending an e-mail, there is a header to every message that contains the following details:

To: In this space, you enter the e-mail address of the person you want to communicate with. This person is normally called the recipient.

Cc: There may be recipients who you want to copy the message to. This is the space used for the carbon copy.

Bcc: Other recipients of the message will not see the name of the recipient in the Blind carbon copy text area.

Subject: This section is used to type a subject relevant to the content of the message.

Attachments: File attachments can be documents, picture, video or sound files sent along with your message.

Body: The main body of the e-mail contains the message itself.

Once your message has been written in the Body section, the e-mail address of the recipient has been typed in the **To:** section, a title for the e-mail has been given in the **Subject:** section, press the **Send** button.

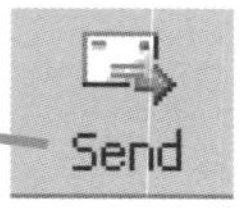

Fig 219

The Internet

The Internet is a system of computers connected together to allow your computer to exchange data, transfer files and communicate messages with other computers connected to the Internet.

The Internet has uses both for business and entertainment. For educational and research purposes, information is published by the Government online, and ranges from OFSTED school inspection reports to Met Office ozone measurements. Schools and colleges are relying more and more on material published on the Internet. There are books, magazine articles and all kinds of reference material readily available to use.

For entertainment you can shop, search, chat, date, advertise and even check film times at your local cinema. The end result is an electronic link to the world of information and entertainment (Fig 220).

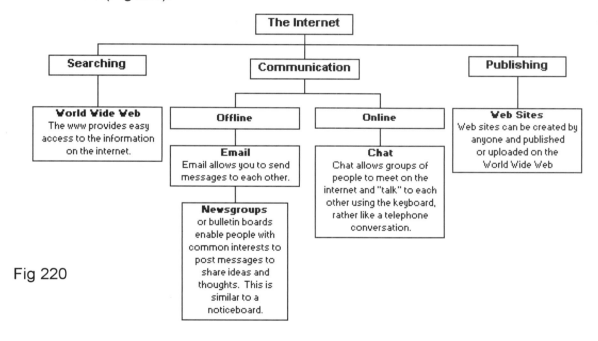

Fig 220

Computer Hardware For Access To The Internet

Before you can access the World Wide Web, you need to be connected to the Internet. There are a number of routes by which to gain access. The company you work for or the college/university that you study at may provide computers that give direct access to the Internet. A cybercafe or public library is yet another option. However, the most versatile method would be to access the Internet through your own computer by setting up an account with an Internet Service Provider (ISP).

Essentially, you need the following pieces of equipment and software to establish a dial-up connection to the Internet:

A computer - Internet Explorer is available for PCs, Apple Macintoshes and Unix workstations, but for the purposes of this pack we'll concentrate on the version for PCs running Windows. As a minimum requirement you will need a computer with a 350 MHz processor, 64 MB of RAM and 500 Mb of free hard disk space. A faster, more powerful computer with more RAM will make browsing the Internet quicker and ultimately more enjoyable.

A modem - There are two types of modem: internal (one that's fitted into your computer) and external (a modem that's attached to a port on your computer). Although modems come in a variety of speeds, anything less than 56 Kbps (kilobits per second) will have you struggling to connect to the Internet. Slower modems may be cheaper, but you'll almost certainly run up a larger phone bill.

A telephone line - Most phone companies offer cheap deals on local calls, making it all the more economical to use the Internet to access all the information you need.

An Internet Service Provider (ISP) - An ISP has a computer system that is permanently connected to the Internet and to a 'bank' of modems. When connecting to the Internet, you use your modem to connect to one of your ISP's modems via your telephone line, thereby making your computer (temporarily) part of the Internet.

Connection software - On your own PC, you will need to install the **Dial-up Networking** utility supplied with Windows to connect to the Internet. You will also require the **Internet Explorer** web browser software to view the web pages once you have established a connection.

T A S K		
	1.	What does the 'e' in 'e-mail' stand for?
	2.	What does the e-mail acronym 'Cc' stand for?
		Only perform the following task if you have access to Outlook Express - if you are unsure please ask your tutor.
	3.	Access the **Outlook Express** application and open a **New** message window.
	4.	Write the following message in the body section:
		E-mail is a very versatile medium. Formats range from simple text to HTML & rich media. Content can be one-size-fits-all or highly customised.
	5.	Type the following e-mail address in the **To:** text area: **equals7@tektra-connect.co.uk**
	6.	Send the e-mail message.
	7.	Name three items that are necessary for connection to the Internet.
		Check your answers on page 173.

The World Wide Web

The **World Wide Web (WWW)** is a collection of web pages that can be viewed using the Internet. The combination of the Internet and the World Wide Web is commonly known as the Information Superhighway. There is an enormous amount of information available on the World Wide Web, such as electronic libraries, weather reports, newspapers, stock market prices, currency exchange rates, government information, hotel accommodation – whatever you can think of, it is there, growing daily as more and more information is made available. You are able to shop anywhere in the world as well as do all your banking via the Internet.

It is likely that in the very near future every school will be connected to the Internet, as will a large proportion of homes. Businesses will depend more and more on the Internet for advertising, sales and information exchange.

To explore the Internet you need a software package called a web browser. Microsoft Internet Explorer and Netscape Navigator are the two most common browsers. The browser software will allow you to search (surf) the Web and access newsgroups and chat rooms.

Fig 221

A browser will enable your computer to display web pages. These web pages are written in a special language called HTML (Hypertext Mark-up Language).

The Web uses the Hypertext Transfer Protocol (HTTP) to download web pages to the browser and TCP/IP (Transmission Control Protocol/Internet Protocol) to allow information to travel between networks.

Web sites often have links to other web pages. These links are known as hyperlinks and contain the address for the web page. These addresses are known as URLs (Uniform Resource Locators) and are unique to each web page.

If you do not know if a particular web site exists or the address or URL of a required web site, you can use a search engine to help you find it. Commonly used search engines are Alta Vista, Lycos and Yahoo. The search engine allows you to type in keywords and it looks these words up in its vast database of sites, returning a list of possibilities for you to investigate.

Computers

Computers In The Home

An increasing number of households now have a computer in them, most of which have Internet access. The Internet helps the transferral and communication of information to all. The home computer has many uses for all members of the family:

- Playing games, from simple card games to sophisticated arcade games.
- Accessing the Internet for homework or school projects, and hobbies.
- Internet shopping and banking.
- Home accounts.
- Studying and working from home.
- Sending and receiving e-mails.

Computerised electronic equipment is everywhere to be found in the modern home, from the washing machine and microwave to the central heating system.

Computers At Work Or In Education

Almost all businesses and educational establishments depend on computer technology; even the smallest office uses a word processor. This use of technology in schools, colleges and universities has increased access to learning throughout society. Some typical business and academic uses are:

- Database applications, such as personnel records, client details.
- Letters, memos, faxes, e-mails (word processing applications).
- Stock control and sales analysis (using spreadsheet applications).
- Advertising and marketing (desktop publishing, word processing, websites).
- Accounting and payroll information.
- Computer-aided design (CAD) and robotics.

Large organisations have special systems known as Information Management Systems (IMS) and Database Management Systems (DBMS).

Commercial organisations make use of electronic fund transfer at point-of-sale (EFTPOS), which is the technology that allows customers to pay for goods by credit and debit cards. Payroll is carried out by means of Electronic Funds Transfer (EFT), which transfers money from one bank account to another.

Education is increasingly using computer technology. Teachers and students use the Internet to research topics; spreadsheets and databases are used for student results. Specialised applications packages are being used for art and design, to help teach foreign languages and for music technology.

The medical industry keeps patients' records on computer. Medical scanners use computer technology and it is now possible for surgeons to assist in the performance of operations over the Internet. Opticians use computer technology to help when prescribing glasses.

Air traffic control rooms rely on computer technology; traffic lights have sensors in them to help regulate the flow of traffic; ships use computers for Global Satellite Positioning. Car factories rely on robots to assemble cars.

Whilst computers are ideally suited to tackle mathematical problems with great speed and accuracy, they cannot, however, take on a role where personal skills are involved, such as thinking, counselling and verbal reasoning. It is unlikely that a computer will take the place of your doctor, for example.

Computers In Daily Life

Computers can be found in everyday use almost everywhere.

Banks and building societies have cash machines where cards are used to withdraw cash, check balances or order a statement. The cards hold information about the customer. These machines are known as Automated Teller Machines (ATMs).

Supermarkets use bar code readers at the tills- these readers are input devices - they read the product code on the things you have purchased; the information is used for the customer's bill and for the shop's stock control. This is known as Electronic Point of Sale (EPOS). Bankcards and credit cards can then be used for payment (EFTPOS – discussed previously).

ATM machine

Fig 222

Libraries have computerised databases; the books are scanned when borrowed and scanned again when returned (The scanners are again input devices). Library catalogues are also held on databases. Internet facilities are available in many libraries, as are e-mail and fax.

Airport and railway terminals have computer screens displaying the arrival and departure times.

TASK

1. Name three household appliances that contain computerised equipment.

2. Computers in the home are used for a variety of different tasks. Name three.

3. When thinking of using a computer for a particular task, what should be considered?

4. What does the term 'CAD' stand for?

5. What computerised system is used to chart the location of ships?

6. The 'Information Superhighway' is another term that is used to describe what?

Check your answers on page 173.

Society And Computers

E-commerce

Identifying the world of commerce is quite simple; in its broadest sense it is the exchange of goods and services, usually for money. We see commerce all around us in millions of different forms. When you buy something at a grocery store or a supermarket you are participating in commerce. If you go to work each day for a company that produces a product or offers a service, that is yet another link in the chain of commerce. When you think about commerce in these different ways, you instinctively recognise several different roles:

- Buyers - these are people with money who want to purchase a good or service.
- Sellers - these are the people who offer goods and services to buyers. Sellers are generally recognised in two different forms: retailers who sell directly to consumers and wholesalers or distributors who sell to retailers and other businesses.
- Producers - these are the people who create the products and services that sellers offer to buyers. A producer is always, by necessity, a seller as well. The producer sells the products produced to wholesalers, retailers or directly to the consumer.

With e-commerce (electronic commerce) you find all of the elements previously mentioned, but they change slightly. You must have the following elements to conduct e-commerce:

- A product or service.
- A place to sell the product - in the case of e-commerce a web site might display the products or service.
- A way to get people to come to your web site - advertising.
- A way to accept orders - normally an online form of some sort.
- A way to accept money - normally a merchant account handling credit card payments. This process requires a secure ordering page and a connection to a bank. Or you may use more traditional billing techniques, either online or by post.
- A fulfilment facility to ship products to customers (often outsourceable). In the case of software and information, however, fulfilment can occur over the Web through a file download mechanism.
- A way to accept returns.
- A way to handle warranty claims if necessary.
- A way to provide customer service (often through e-mail, on-line forms, on-line knowledge bases and FAQs - Frequently Asked Questions, etc).

The most essential element of e-commerce is the World Wide Web. Using the Internet commercial transactions that span across the globe take place in a matter of minutes, sometimes even seconds.

The success of e-commerce has come about due to the fact that in the long term it has proved to be faster, more efficient, and ultimately a less costly method of conducting business transactions.

T A S K

1. Explain, in simple terms, the essential difference between commerce and e-commerce.

2. Name two elements that are instrumental in the conduct of e-commerce.

Check your answers on page 173.

Health And Safety

Creating A Good Working Environment

When working with computers it is important to ensure you have a safe and comfortable environment to work in. There are many regulations and standards in place that govern the use of computers. Following thes guidelines and procedures means that problems can be avoided through good work area design and by the way you use your VDU and work area:

- You need to have a well designed chair giving good back and leg support.

- Sit upright and well back in the chair and adjust the height so that your hands are comfortably on the keyboard, with your forearms horizontal and your feet on the ground.

- The keyboard should not be placed too close to the edge of the table, nor is it advisable to rest your wrists on the desk as this can add strain.

Fig 223

- If your keyboard is not designed with wrist support, you can purchase this computer accessory separately.

- Make sure there is enough desk space for the computer and any paperwork you need.

- The computer screen is adjustable and should be positioned at arm's length, with the top of the monitor at about a 40 degree angle to your eyes (see above).

- The screen should be flicker-free and there should be gentle lighting, which does not produce screen glare.

- Use window blinds if necessary.

- There must be adequate ventilation and an even temperature.

- It is important to rest your eyes frequently by focusing on distant objects and take breaks away from the computer during the day.

The previously described procedures will reduce eyestrain, eye damage and visual fatigue, as well as helping to prevent muscle strain in the neck and shoulders. Repetitive strain injury (RSI) is caused by the prolonged use of particular muscles and can affect many parts of your body. This can be avoided by taking breaks away from the computer desk.

Safe Working Practices

It is also important to keep the computer equipment in a safe and clean condition; power cables should be soundly connected and stored securely so they cannot be tripped over; screens should be frequently cleaned; power sockets must be fused, in good working order and not overloaded.

Cleaning Computer Components

Cleaning your computer and your computer components helps keep them in good working condition. You should clean your computer components regularly.

System Unit

The plastic case that houses the PC components can be cleaned with a lint-free cloth. Most computer manufacturers would recommend that you use an anti- static cleaner (specialist substance) or anti static wipes to clean the system unit.

CD-ROM drive

A dirty CD-ROM drive can cause read errors with CD disks not allowing you to install software or causing errors during the installation of software.

To clean the CD-ROM drive it is recommended that you purchase a CD-ROM cleaner available from any reputable electrical retailer vendor. Using a CD-ROM cleaner should sufficiently clean the CD-ROM laser of dust, dirt and hair.

Compact Disk

Cleaning CDs can be accomplished with a CD cleaning kit, but a normal clean cotton cloth or shirt will do just as well. When using a clean cotton cloth or shirt, wipe against the tracks, starting from the middle of the CD and wiping towards the outer side of the CD. Never wipe with the tracks - doing so may put more scratches on the CD. Specialist cleaning materials are available to clean CDs.

When cleaning any of the components on your computer it is important to follow the instructions below

*   Read the manufacturers instructions
*   Read the instructions on the cleaning fluid/materials
*   Do not carry out the cleaning if you are not sure of what to do
*   Ensure that you have switched off the computer (if cleaning the monitor/keyboard/system unit)
*   Be aware of others around you

Floppy Disk

Dirty read/write heads on the floppy disk drive can cause errors during the reading and/or writing process.

The recommended method of cleaning a floppy drive is to purchase a kit at your local retail store designed to clean the read/write heads on your floppy drive.

Hard Drive

While hard drives cannot be cleaned physically, they can be cleaned with various utilities on the computer to help it run faster and more efficiently. Utilising these tools will prevent the hard drive from slowing down.

Running system software programs such as **Scandisk** and **Defrag** will help to organise files and save space on the hard drive.

Keyboard

If the keyboard has had anything spilt onto it, not taking the proper steps can cause the keyboard to be destroyed.

Many people clean the keyboard by turning it upside down and shaking. A more effective method is to use compressed air. Compressed air is pressurized air contained in a can with a very long nozzle. Simply aim the air between the keys and blow away all of the dust and debris that has gathered there.

A vacuum cleaner can also be used, but make sure the keyboard does not have loose keys that could possibly be sucked up by the vacuum cleaner.

The Monitor

The monitor screen can be cleaned with screen wipes or an anti-static spray foam. As with all components that are to be cleaned, ensure the monitor is not switched on.

Remove dirt from the monitor by spraying the cleaner onto a lint-free cloth (and not directly onto the monitor) and applying it evenly over the face of the screen. Vacuum off any dust that has settled on top of the monitor and make sure objects have not been placed over the air vents. Obstructed monitor vents can cause the monitor to overheat or even catch on fire.

Mouse

Sometimes the on-screen mouse pointer may be difficult to control. This is usually caused by a collection of dust and dirt that the mouse picks up from the surface of your desk or mouse mat.

To clean the rollers of a mouse you must first remove the bottom cover of the mouse. To do this, examine the bottom of the mouse to see in which direction the mouse cover should be rotated. As you can see in Fig 224, the mouse cover must be moved anti-clockwise. Place two fingers on the mouse cover and push in the direction of the arrows.

Fig 224

Once the ball has been removed from the mouse, use your finger and/or fingernail and move in a horizontal direction along the rollers. Usually there will be a small line of hair and or dirt in the middle of the roller. Remove this dirt and or hair as often as possible. Special swabs can be puchased to do this rather than using your fingers.

Once you have removed as much dirt and hair as possible, place the ball back within the mouse and place the cover back on.

Computers And Legal Requirements

Fatigue, muscular aches and strains, eye strain etc are common symptoms for all users of computer keyboards, mouse and display equipment, particularly when intensive use is coupled with occasional tasks. These common and usually short-lived symptoms can develop into more serious and long-lasting effects in some individuals which, in extreme cases, may lead to severe impairment of both work and leisure activities.

Management Of Health And Safety At Work Regulations

The assessment and management of VDU usage is covered in the Health & Safety (Display Screen Equipment) Regulations (1992). Here, employers are required to:

- Assess each workstation in the context of each user.
- Review the assessment whenever necessary.
- Reduce risks identified to the lowest extent reasonably practicable.
- Plan activities of users to allow periodic breaks/changes of activity.
- Ensure that users are entitled to an appropriate eye test on request. Further tests to be carried out at regular intervals. Tests to be carried out if user has visual difficulties in using display screen. Employer to supply glasses if necessary.
- Ensure that users and forthcoming users are trained in use of workstations and to ensure that users are retrained when workstations are substantially modified.
- Provide adequate information to operators and users on all aspects of health and safety related to their workstations and measures taken to comply with regulations.

Hazardous Substances

Health and Safety Inspectors make sure that all employers are following the COSHH regulations - The Care of Substances Hazardous to Health. These regulations are about the storage, handling and disposal of hazardous substances. Substances that are hazardous are clearly marked with a warning symbol together with any special instructions.

Examples of common warning symbols:

harmful   flammable   toxic   corrosive   explosive
or Irritant

When using computers the most likely hazards are from toner used in printers and photocopiers, which is a fine dust. Careful handling requires the use of gloves and special waste disposal. Inhalation should be avoided, as should contact with skin. It is always advisable to check the manufacturer's instructions.

Cleaning fluids and some fluids used in reprographic processes are flammable. Always handle these with care and store in minimum quantities, preferably in metal, away from heat. Other substances, such as solvents, are dangerous to inhale. Care should always be taken to re-seal lids securely and store in upright containers. They should not be used in confined spaces and adequate ventilation should be maintained.

Health & Safety At Work Act 1974

The Health & Safety At Work Act 1974 requires employers to ensure, as far as possible, the health and safety of its employees. An employee also has duties under the Act to take reasonable care of their own health and safety and that of others; co-operate with employers; correctly use work items and not interfere or misuse anything provided for their health and safety.

Steps to take to ensure your safety and the safety of others:

- Do not allow trailing cables and wires to create a tripping hazard.
- Power sockets should not be overloaded.
- Clear up spillages quickly.
- Report safety hazards such as torn or worn carpets to the appropriate person.
- Do not block passageways and fire exits.
- Work in a safe manner at all times.
- Keep your work area tidy and free from hazards.

T A S K

Answer the following questions:

1. Look at the picture below of a work area and identify at least four potential hazards:

2. Which regulation covers the care of hazardous substances?

3. The Health & Safety At Work Act 1974 only sets out duties for the employer. Is this statement true or false?

4. It is a good idea to rest your wrists on the desk. Is this statement true or false?

5. To maintain safe working practices it is important that you work:

   a) quickly.
   b) without disturbing others.
   c) in a safe manner at all times.
   d) with harmful substances.

Check your answers on page 174.

Security

Security

Data security is very important for all businesses and users as the loss of major files can have extremely serious consequences. The main causes of data loss are:

- Fire, flood and other natural accidents.
- Mechanical problems such as a faulty disk drive.
- Software errors, human error or malicious damage.

Back Ups

By keeping regular back up copies of your data and storing these back ups in a safe and separate place away from the computer, you will ensure that you have duplicate copies of your files in the event of a disaster. Back ups are exact copies of your data and can be stored on removable disks, CD-RW, tapes or zip drives. There are various back up programs available, some of which also compress your data, reducing the amount of storage space required.

Passwords

Your computer and the data held can be safeguarded with the use of passwords. Individual files can be password-protected and highly confidential data can require several passwords before access is allowed.

Passwords should be regularly changed and should ideally be alphanumeric (a mixture of letters and numbers) and should use both upper and lower case characters. They should not be meaningful words that could be guessed by others. Passwords should never be divulged to anyone other than authorised users.

If you experience a power cut whilst using the computer, data and information that has not been saved will unfortunately be lost. It is therefore important to save your work regularly, say, every 10 minutes, so that you reduce the time you will need to redo the work lost. Some software applications have automatic back ups that occur in the background and when the computer is restarted they will attempt to load the last saved back up. Sometimes a computer will suddenly stop functioning of its own accord and this is known as a system crash. When this happens the computer will have to be restarted. Any data not saved since the last back up will be lost.

TASK

1. Give two examples for the possible cause of data loss.

2. Name two external back up devices for storing your data.

3. What is the term for when a computer suddenly stops working of its own accord?

Check your answers on page 174.

Ways In Which Viruses Are Distributed

A virus is a program that duplicates itself from one file to another without consent. For example, a virus might attach itself to a program such as a spreadsheet program. Each time the spreadsheet program runs, the virus runs too, and it has the chance to reproduce by attaching to other programs. Some of the most common viruses are:

E-mail viruses - An e-mail virus moves around attached to e-mail messages, and usually replicates itself by automatically mailing itself to dozens of people in the victim's e-mail address book (for example the *I Love You* virus that had a devastating effect on e-mail systems in 2000).

Worms - A worm is a small piece of software that uses computer networks and security holes to replicate itself. A copy of the worm scans the network for another machine that has a specific security hole. It copies itself to the new machine using the security hole, and then starts replicating from there, as well. These may be placed on a network by a malicious user or brought onto a network attached to a file or e-mail.

Trojans- A Trojan is simply a computer program. The program claims to do one thing (it may claim to be a game) but instead does damage when you run it (it may erase your hard disk for example). Trojans have no way of replicating automatically.

Macro virus - A macro virus is spread on applications which use macros. The macro viruses which are receiving attention currently are specific to Word and Excel. However, many applications, not all of them Windows applications, have potentially damaging and infective macro capabilities too.

Viruses are distributed in various ways:

- A script attached to e-mail messages.
- Within an executable program.
- Transferred by a malicious user (hacker).
- As a macro within a document.

The key defence is regular file back up and prevention is by the use of firewalls and other active anti-virus monitoring software. Regularly updated anti-virus packages are also capable of removing or neutralising some existing virus infections.

Anti-virus Software

Every computer should be running up-to-date anti-virus software. Preferably one should be used that will scan any files which are being downloaded to your system or which have been sent to you via e-mail, as this is where many viruses are aimed and how they are spread to others.

It is important to have up-to-date software of this type as new viruses are being written every day. The more up-to-date your software is, the better the chance of cleaning the infected files. After all, prevention is better than cure in this case.

T
A
S
K

1. In your own words, describe what a computer virus is and what it can do to your computer.

2. Explain what a Trojan is.

3. What special circumstances are needed for a worm to replicate itself?

4. Explain how an e-mail virus is spread.

5. Passwords are used to:

   a) download e-mail messages.
   b) safeguard data held on a computer.
   c) check the time spent on the computer.
   d) play games.

6. An effective defence against viruses is to install a:

   a) fire fighter.
   b) hacker.
   c) firewall.
   d) brickwall.

7. It is recommended that work is saved every:

   a) 60 minutes.
   b) 20 minutes.
   c) 10 minutes.
   d) day.

Check your answers on page 175.

Fire Precautions

It is imperative that wherever you work, in whatever profession, fire safety regulations are adhered to by your employer so that all work premises are safe and healthy environments for all employees.

The Fire Precautions (Workplace) Regulations, as amended in 1997, covers places of work where one or more persons are employed, eg commercial premises, universities, hospitals, shops, hotels and offices.

The amended regulations state that premises with over five workers must have a written fire risk assessment detailing the appropriate fire safety work required.

Following the fire risk assessment the employer must, where necessary in order to safeguard the safety of employees in case of fire and to the extent that it is appropriate, provide:

- Emergency exit routes and doors.

- Final emergency exit doors that must open outwards and not be sliding or revolving.

- Emergency lighting to cover the exit routes, where necessary.

- Fire-fighting equipment, fire alarms and, where necessary, fire detectors.

Fire Exit signs, fire alarms and fire-fighting equipment must be provided with pictograph signs - Health and Safety (Safety Signs & Signals) Regulations 1996.

Employers must train employees in fire safety following the written risk assessment. An emergency plan may have to be prepared and sufficient workers trained and equipped to carry out their functions within any such plan.

All equipment and facilities such as fire extinguishers, alarms systems and emergency doors should be regularly maintained and faults rectified as soon as possible. Defects and repairs must be recorded.

Employers must plan, organise, control, monitor and review the measures taken to protect employees from fire whilst at work and if there are more than five employees, then a record must be maintained.

Regarding Fire Precaution Regulations in the workplace, the issues mentioned only cover the main points of fire safety in the workplace.

Although the issues raised may seem like quite a lot of information to take in, if employers intentionally or recklessly fail to comply they will be guilty of an offence.

Copyright

Software is protected by copyright laws. When you purchase a software application you are also purchasing the licence required to run that software on your computer. By loading the software you are entering an agreement with the manufacturer to use it for personal use only and not to copy it (except for your personal back up) or lend it to anyone else.

Freeware is software that is freely available and can be used free of charge. It is often given away with computer magazines or it can be downloaded from the Internet.

Shareware is software that is available free of charge for evaluation purposes. There is usually a time limit for you to try out the software, after which if you wish to continue using it you should register your copy and pay for the licence. Shareware is also distributed with magazines and downloaded from the Internet.

Data Protection Act

The Data Protection Act came into force in 1984 and was updated on 1 March 2000. The Data Protection Act identifies eight principles to safeguard personal information stored about individuals. The Data Protection Act covers data held on computer files and some paper-based files. It also gives individuals the right to see the records held about them, with the exception of police records and some medical records.

Any organisation that holds computerised personal data must register with the Data Protection Registrar as a data user and they must state the purpose for which they wish to hold the data.

Personal data is kept for many reasons – personnel records, tax records, banks records, credit worthiness, medical records. In all cases the data must comply with the following principles to ensure it is handled correctly.

The data must be:

- Fairly and lawfully processed.
- Processed for limited purposes.
- Adequate, relevant and not excessive
- Accurate.
- Not kept for longer than is necessary.
- Processed in line with your rights.
- Secure.
- Not transferred to other countries without adequate protection.

NB   These rules apply to the UK only. Other countries will have their own Data Protection Act.

T A S K

1.   Shareware is:

   a) software that is free of charge.
   b) software purchased with a licence.
   c) software available for evaluation purpose, after which you register and pay for the licence.
   d) software freely available to be copied.

2.   Software is protected by:

   a) a licence.
   b) the owners.
   c) copyright laws.
   d) the Internet.

Check your answers on page 175.

Appendix

IT Principles Glossary

Application	A computer program that performs specific tasks such as manipulating text, numerical analysis and design etc.
Backup	A copy of a program or data file that is kept for archive purposes. This is usually stored on a removable floppy or hard disk.
Bus	A channel through which data passes.
CPU	Central Processing Unit. The core of a computer system containing the integrated circuits that are required to interpret and execute instructions and perform basic computer functions.
Data	Information such as groups of facts, symbols, letters, numbers or instructions that are used to communicate and make decisions.
Default	A pre-set preference used by programs. For example, the operating system may use a default printer to print to.
Desktop	The operating system environment that uses a Graphical User Interface (GUI). It is a graphical representation of the top of a desk onto which files and folders can be kept.
Directory	The contents of a computer file system allowing convenient access to specified files. A directory is an area of the disk that stores files. They are used as a file management system.
E-commerce	Business transactions carried out over a computer network.
E-mail	The use of Networks of computers to send and receive messages. It has the ability to connect groups of people on a worldwide basis.
Extensions	A representation on the end of a file such as .doc to determine with which program a file will operate with.
Facsimile	A device that enables the transmitting and receiving of an exact copy of a page of printed data over telephone lines.
File	A collection of data or information that is given a specific name and is saved on the computers storage facility.
Folder	Otherwise known as a Directory in which files are located and stored. Folders are represented on screen by icons and can be related to folders in a filing cabinet.
Heirarchy	The branching structure of files and folders (directories) in Windows Explorer.

Internet	A worldwide system of linked computer networks. Computers can be linked that have different operating systems.
LAN	Local Area Network. A group of personal computers all linked via cables within a local area. Users are then able to share the same printer and files and folders.
Multimedia	The combining of computer data, sound and video images creating an image similar to television.
Pixel	The smallest dot that can be displayed on a screen. Pixels make up the picture that is displayed on the screen.
Program	A set of instructions that make a digital computer perform a designated operation.
RAM	Random Access Memory. This can be classed as the main memory or internal memory. RAM stores program instructions and data to make them available to the CPU.
Resolution	A measurement of the sharpness of an image on a printer or a VDU (Screen). Resolution is measured in 'dots per inch'. The more dots per inch the greater the sharpness of the image on paper.
ROM	Read Only Memory. The part of a computer's internal memory which can be read but not altered or erased. Contains essential program information.
Run	To execute a program.
Shortcut	Either a key combination to allow users to bypass the normal menu's to perform specific tasks faster, or a link to a specific file or folder.
Start (button)	The operating system (Microsoft Windows) starting point to open specific programs from the Desktop environment.
System	All the necessary hardware and software required to make up a computer system. All of this equipment connected together.
Virus	A program written specifically to cause damage to systems that it effects. Viruses can spread very fast from file to file or from disk to disk. They can also pass between computer systems through infected disks and communication systems.
WAN	Wide Area Network. A computer network that connects computers over long distances using the telephone lines or satellites.
Zip	A method of compressing files to enable them to take up less space on a disk.

Answers

Page 44

1.   21 cm x 29.7 cm.

2.   200°c.

3.   14.85 cm.

Page 46

1.   32.3 cm x 22.9 cm.

2.   12 - 14 per sheet.

3.   A4 labels, CD-ROM labels, circular adhesive labels.

Page 49

1.   21.9 cm x 11 cm.

2.   100mm x 38mm.

3.   A4 address labels – placed on envelopes. CD-ROM label and circular adhesive label.

4.   A3 – 29.7 cm x 42 cm.
      A4 – 21 cm x 29.7 cm.
      A5 – 14.85 cm x 21 cm.

5.   Melt or release hazardous emissions.

6.   Two from the following: envelopes, cards, labels, transparencies.

7.   Floppy disk or CD-ROM.

8.   Ensure all packaging and sealant tape have been removed. Gently shake the print cartridge from side to side to distribute the toner evenly.

Page 58

1.   Two from the following: Check printer has a transparency option in the Properties dialogue box. Use transparencies designed specifically for your printer. Avoid getting fingerprints on the transparencies. Fan the stack to prevent the sheets from sticking together.

Page 67

1.   Program files and data files.

2.   Two from the following: .bin, .exe, .sea, .tar, .zip.

3.   Netscape Navigator or Internet Explorer.

4.   Compressed and encoded files.

Page 87

3.   .mp3 and .wav

4.   Video files.

5.   Graphics files

Page 134 – Task

1.   Random Access Memory.

2.   3½"

3.   1.44 Mb

Page 134 – Consolidation

1.   8

2.   1.44 Mb

3.   3½"

4.   Two of the following: CD-ROM, zip disk, data cartridge, CD-R/CD-RW, DVD.

5.   Random access memory is the short-term memory or working and Read-only memory holds program instructions permanently that cannot be altered.

6.   To avoid losing data.

7.   The type of processor and its speed. The amount of RAM available.

8.   Magnetic disks, magnetic tape, optical storage.

Page 145

1.   Asynchronous Transfer Mode.

2.   Digital Subscriber Line.

3.   Local Area Network.

4.   Wide Area Network.

5.   Integrated Services Digital Network.

6.   Modulator/demodulator.

7.   Refers to any type of transmission technique that carries several data channels over a common wire.

Page 150

1.   Electronic.

2.   Carbon copy.

7.   Three from the following: computer, modem, telephone line, ISP, connection and browser software.

Page 154

1.   Washing machine, microwave, central heating system.

2.   Three from the following: playing games; accessing the Internet for homework; shopping and banking; home accounts; studying and working from home; sending and receiving e-mails.

3.   Is a computer really necessary or is it being used because that is what is expected.

4.   Computer-aided design.

5.   Global satellite positioning.

6.   The combination of the Internet and the World Wide Web.

Page 156

1.   Commerce is the exchange of goods and services, usually for money. E-commerce has the same elements as commerce but is based on the World Wide Web.

2. Two from the following: a product or service; a web site to sell the produce; advertising; online ordering; a way to accept money; a fulfilment facility to ship products to customers; a way to accept returns; a way to handle warranty claims if necessary; a way to provide customer service.

Page 162

1.

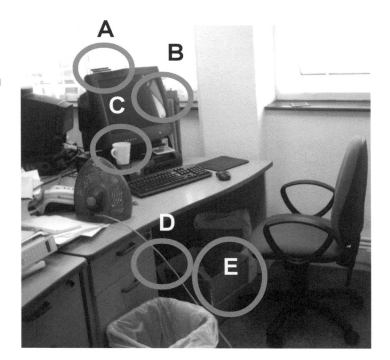

A   Hazard from falling items balancing on VDU screen

B   Glare on screen

C   Cup on base unit

D   Trailing wire

E   Boxes causing an obstruction under desk

2   COSHH - Control of Substances Hazardous to Health

3. False

4. False

5. C

Page 163

1. Fire, flood and other natural accidents; mechanical problems; software errors; human error or malicious damage.

2. CD-RW, tapes or zip drives.

3. System crash.

Page 165

1. A computer virus is a hidden file with a series of commands. They can be destructive or reproduce themselves.

2. A Trojan horse is a computer virus in the form of a computer program which causes damage when run. They do not replicate automatically.

3. A worm needs to find a security hole.

4. E-mail viruses are spread through attachments. E-mails are automatically sent to addresses in the address book.

5. b

6. c

7. c

Page 167

1. c

2. c